# QUEER IN BLACK AND WHITE

# QUEER IN BLACK AND WHITE

## INTERRACIALITY, SAME SEX DESIRE, AND CONTEMPORARY AFRICAN AMERICAN CULTURE

STEFANIE K. DUNNING

Indiana University Press
*Bloomington and Indianapolis*

This book is a publication of

Indiana University Press
601 North Morton Street
Bloomington, IN 47404–3797 USA

http://iupress.indiana.edu

| *Telephone orders* | 800–842–6796 |
| *Fax orders* | 812–855–7931 |
| *Orders by e-mail* | iuporder@indiana.edu |

Manufactured in the United States of America

*Library of Congress Cataloging-in-Publication Data*

Dunning, Stefanie K., date
    Queer in black and white : interraciality, same sex desire, and contemporary African American culture / Stefanie K. Dunning.
        p.    cm.
    Includes bibliographical references and index.
    ISBN 978-0-253-35350-4 (cloth : alk. paper)—
    ISBN 978-0-253-22109-4 (pbk. : alk. paper)
        1. American fiction—African American authors—History and criticism.
    2. African Americans—Intellectual life. 3. Homosexuality in literature
    4. Homosexuality in motion pictures. 5. Homosexuality in music. 6. Race
    relations in literature. 7. Race relations in motion pictures. 8. African
    Americans—Race identity. I. Title.
        PS153.N5D86   2009
        700'.452664—dc22

                                                         2008053533

1   2   3   4   5   14   13   12   11   10   09

*I would like to dedicate this book to those*
*who brought me here but have now gone on.*

John Steven Dunning

Elizabeth Frazier

Garrett Frazier

Sandra Dunning LaBoria

# CONTENTS

# ACKNOWLEDGMENTS

The players on the stage of the psychic drama that this book has been are many, and all were important in its becoming. I thank you all. This book, like so many inaugural books in an academic's career, began as a dissertation. The Ford Foundation fellowship I received as a graduate student undoubtedly helped in my formulation of the dissertation, parts of which are present within these pages. I would like to thank the Ford Foundation for all of its support through the years, not only during my graduate student years but afterward as well. I would also like to thank everyone at Indiana University Press, but especially my editor, Bob Sloan, for his guidance and patience. I also thank Anne Clemmer for all of her assistance regarding the images used in this book.

I must recognize my dissertation committee for the work they did to help me formulate this project. Professors Jennifer DeVere Brody, Parama Roy, and Carole-Anne Tyler were instrumental in the genesis of this project, and their insights, suggestions, and criticism were invaluable. I admire them all and am profoundly glad that they have been part of my life. I am indebted to many wonderful friends and colleagues as well. For helping me come up with a new title for this book, I am forever beholden to my longtime friend and colleague Candice Jenkins. She tirelessly read (and listened to me read) countless drafts and spent hours discussing the finer points of the book with me. I would especially like to thank to Mary Jean Corbett, who read this manuscript in its entirety and offered thorough comments and suggestions for correction and revision. This book would not be what it is without her careful, methodical, and insightful eye. Thanks also go to Cheryl Johnson for keeping me sane, for proofing chapter 1, and for always playing devil's advocate. And to Katie Johnson for her constant support and friendship as well as her insightful comments on the film *The Watermelon Woman*. I would also like to thank Siobhan Somerville for her advice and continued support. My heartfelt thanks go to Robert Reid-Pharr for reading chapter 1 of this manuscript as well as for his service to me as a colleague. I would also like to thank Amrijit Singh for his comments on the Harlem Renaissance, and Deb Meem for her thoughtful engagement with this book.

To all of my colleagues at Miami University, many of whom have enriched my life in ways they probably aren't even aware of, I offer my appreciation. I would like to mention Kate Ronald, who always knows exactly what to say; Gwen Etter-Lewis, for validating my sense of reality and for reading an early draft of the introduction; Barry Chabot, whose belief in me sustains me even now; Susan Morgan, whose example gives me courage to speak; Fran Dolan, whose kindness I will never forget, and for her input on chapter 1; Tim Melley, for all of our many interesting discussions; and Madelyn Detloff, for her simple, but completely true, early advice. If I had followed it, I'd have been writing these acknowledgments much sooner.

In addition to my friends and colleagues, I'd like to acknowledge a few people who played a more indirect role in the publication of this book. I must give credit to Crystal Haymes, a positively amazing child-care provider, who came into our lives and transformed everything for the better. Without her cheerful, reliable, and excellent child care, I would not have been able to complete this project. I would also like to thank my daughter, Ayomi. Though she cannot yet read this, I hope she one day realizes that the joy she brings to my life every day sustains me in ways that make writing possible. I would also like to thank my family for all the many ways they encourage and support me, especially my brother Christopher Dunning, whose example inspires me and makes me proud.

Finally, I must thank Nalin Jayasena. He has seen this project, and me, transform since I first began work on what would ultimately become *Queer in Black and White* in 1999. His support, in many areas of my life, has enabled this project. For his perseverance and love, I am eternally grateful.

# QUEER IN BLACK AND WHITE

*It's true! There ain't no good black men out there. They're either in jail, drug addicts, homos . . . the good ones know they the shit, so they got ten women at a time, leaving babies all over the place.*

*—Jungle Fever*

*Black men loving Black men is THE revolutionary act!*

*—Tongues Untied*

According to the women in Spike Lee's film *Jungle Fever* (1991), good black men are not gay. And being gay is akin to being a drug addict, a criminal, and a rolling stone. The other problem these women are discussing is black men dating white women. One woman in the group (in fact, the one quoted in the first epigraph above) suggests that black women should forget skin color and date white men. She is booed by the group; her interracial solution to their problems is dismissed.¹ After indicating that she would never date a white man, one woman argues that for black men, "their responsibility level is not the same as ours." This woman sees "our" responsibility as one of nation building, of commitment to the black family—a commitment these particular characters profess allegiance to despite their personal pain and hardship. As the black woman jilted for a white lover argues, "My marriage is wrecked . . . the man is gone and *I* still believe there are good black men out there." While black men are being criticized for failing the nation, the black women refuse to flee the homestead. They do so to their own detriment, ironically defining their needs as outside the respectable bounds of a community which they increasingly see themselves as occupying alone. They lament that as black women they are "losing their men." The equation of interracial desire and gay identity connects queer identity to that which is outside. Like the white women who take their men away from them, so too does being gay make black men unavailable to black women and hence to the black nation.

Though queer identity is never discussed again in *Jungle Fever*, this moment illustrates the way mainstream black discourse defines black queer identity as untenable to a normalized black identity while at the same time pathologizing it (aligning it with drug addiction and criminality) and connecting it to interracial desire and to whiteness. The idea that to be queer is to be outside the black community is one of the central claims that much black queer theory, as well as this book, contests. We can trace this notion in the contemporary moment most notably to the Black Arts Movement of the 1960s. The nationalist ethos which underpins this scene in *Jungle Fever* owes its ideology in large part to the rejection of black gay and lesbian identity professed most notably by Amiri Baraka, Eldridge Cleaver, and other black nationalists of the 1960s and '70s.

Given this negative characterization of what it means to be black and queer, it is perhaps surprising that contemporary black queer texts would stage, confront, and interrogate the interracial as much as they do. Yet some of the most significant texts about black queer identity consciously and unambiguously represent interracial desire. *Queer in Black and White* is an examination of a series of those texts. All of the texts examined in *Queer in Black and White* are important to the nascent canon of black gay and lesbian studies (many of them are "firsts"), as well as by their attention to homosexuality and interraciality. Among the texts I analyze in this volume are *Plantation Lullabies* (1993), composed by Me'Shell NdegéOcello, the first "out" hip-hop artist; Cheryl Dunye's *The Watermelon Woman* (1997), the first feature-length film about black lesbian identity; and Ann Allen Shockley's largely ignored novel *Loving Her* (1974), the first novel by an African American about a black lesbian, which is often compared to Radclyffe Hall's *The Well of Loneliness* (1928), the first lesbian novel ever published. I also discuss *Tongues Untied* (1991), which was one of the first filmic explorations of gay black male life from the perspective of a gay black male director, Marlon Riggs. Similarly, though James Baldwin's *Another Country* was not the first novel to represent a black gay (or bisexual) man,[2] it is one of the texts in black queer studies that is most widely read and broadly commented on (from Eldridge Cleaver to Robert Reid-Pharr).

The second epigraph that opens this introduction at once rejects the logic of the black women's conversation in *Jungle Fever*, while simultaneously embracing a similar ideology of intraracial love as redemption. The evocative statement appears in at least two places in black queer discourse—in a poem by Joseph Beam and in *Tongues Untied*. In the film, this declaration follows Riggs's confession of his preference for white lovers. Riggs's progress through this autobiographical film is relatively linear, moving from the crisis of intraracial homophobia in childhood, to racism in the white gay community in adulthood, and then finally into the monoracial, same-sex community of black gay men. Though *Tongues Untied* gracefully navigates the homophobia of the black community and the racism of the gay community to arrive at same-race, same-sex love as the solution to the interstitial dilemma faced by black gay men, such a precise ending was not to be had in Riggs's own life. Given the intimately autobiographical nature of the film, it hardly seems a violation of authorial fallacy to point out that Riggs's lifelong partner was a white man. My goal here, however, is not to call Riggs out. I am not attempting to, as we used to say in the language of my youth, "front." Instead, what I would like to suggest is that this incongruity between what is professed in *Tongues Untied* and what happened in Riggs's life signals a strategy around interracial desire in black queer texts that opposes the logic of black nationalism so evident in the *Jungle Fever* scene referred to above. In other words, the second epigraph should be read not so much as a policing of desire but rather as a political structure of identification. This, I hope to show throughout this book, is the work that the interracial performs in the black queer texts I examine in *Queer in Black and White*.

If, in a world that perpetually silences the black queer subject, there is such a thing as a black queer canon,[3] then *Tongues Untied* is undoubtedly one of its most important texts. The film aired on PBS as part of its *P.O.V.* series in 1991 and was one of the first texts about black gay life to reach a broad American viewership.[4] Available to any American with a television, Riggs's film was one of the first texts by an African American to stage black gay desire in the "mainstream marketplace."[5] Riggs's treatment of interraciality *topographizes* the historicity of cross-racial romance, exposes the tyranny of imposing a politics of authenticity on desire, and at once embraces and rejects the competing narratives which frame, produce, and hinder interraciality in black art through the productively contradictory nature of its text ("Black men loving black men is . . .") and subtext (Riggs's "real" life partner). The dynamic tension between the text and subtext of *Tongues Untied* indeed *preserves* multiple narratives about, and disallows the unequivocal repudiation of, interracial desire. Before turning to a closer reading of Riggs's film, though, I'd like to make some comments on the issues of authenticity, same-sex desire, and the tradition of interraciality in the African American literary tradition which frames the counter-discourse of black queer signifying on the interracial.[6]

## Black Nation, Queer Nation

Contemporary notions of black identity, and the rise of black nationalism after the successes of the civil rights movement, are marked by self-assurance rather than insecurity about racial identity. If we could call the narratives of the first hundred years of African American literature explorations which asked questions about who is black and what it means to be black,[7] then much of the literature produced after 1950 seems more interested in rigidifying black identity than in representing it as mutable. This shift toward the articulation of a particular kind of black identity is evidenced by the work and ideology of the Black Arts Movement.[8] During the Black Arts Movement, figures like Amiri Baraka were eager to define black identity, and one thing black identity was not, according to Baraka, was queer. Amiri Baraka's phobic rhetoric and Eldridge Cleaver's screed against the "negro homosexual" prefigured contemporary black homophobia, rendering gay identity contrary to an "authentic" political black identity. As E. Patrick Johnson notes, "Baraka's rhetoric necessitates the founding of blackness on heterosexual masculinity."[9] Speaking about this exclusion in his essay "Loyalty," Essex Hemphill writes:

> The Black homosexual is hard pressed to gain audience among his heterosexual brothers . . . This is what the race has depended on in being able to erase homosexuality from our recorded history . . . [But] we will not go away with our issues of sexuality. We are coming home.[10]

Hemphill's comment simultaneously embodies the black queer's ostracism from the black community and also, paradoxically, the abiding sense of that community as "home." Undergirding Hemphill's clinging to and investment in the idea of home is a black nationalist ethos. Black nationalism is a powerful force that enabled significant gains for black people, and, of course, it has a long and complicated history (to be discussed in more detail in the chapters to follow), which is part of what makes it impossible for the black subject to completely disavow. But despite that progress, one of the problems with black nationalism was the authenticating discourses it used to "otherize" black queers. Much has been made of the discourses of authenticity that seek to exclude the black queer subject from the nation.[11] Black queer theory has deconstructed at length the rendering of queer sexuality as a "white disease."[12]

"Coming home" means having it out. It means confronting the arguments that keep one on the other side of the gate. Hence contemporary black nationalism structures discourses about interraciality in some of the black queer canon's most important texts. In order to counter the narrative propagated by Baraka and his ilk, the black queer subject has to confront the implications of the idea that queer identity is not *a black thing*. The attempt to exclude black gays and lesbians from the African American community requires that black queer texts devote a tremendous amount of attention to the idea of "the black community" and nationalism. This complicated contestation of black nationalist homophobia, and the simultaneous grappling with racism, motivates the coupling of interraciality and same-sex desire in the texts I examine in *Queer in Black and White*. It is this concern with the black nation which frames these representations of cross-racial, same-sex desire.

One way for us to read the representation of the interracial in black queer texts is to see it as a signal that marks an affirmation of black subjectivity. Interracial desire in the black, same-sex text builds upon the African American literary tradition's representation of the interracial. In this way, black queer texts that represent interraciality historicize themselves along a continuum of African American literary representations of miscegenation. And like the many texts which are referenced in the signifying of miscegenation[13] in the black queer context, the function of the interracial in these texts is to reframe and solidify blackness. The stakes of a claim to blackness, however, are different in the black queer text. While earlier representations of interraciality sought to define blackness against the larger context of American culture, black queer texts speak at once *against* the larger culture and—most importantly—*within* the black community. Using the interracial as a site to stage and highlight blackness, these black queer texts suggest that blackness is not undermined by queerness, which explicitly critiques the idea that to be queer is to collude with whiteness. Even when interracial texts seem on the surface to disavow blackness, we can see the retention of black identity.[14]

At stake in my argument is a rejection of the notion that queer identity is a "white disease" and that to be gay or lesbian or bisexual or transgender is to be outside the race. It might seem, at least to one with nationalist sensibilities, that asserting one's blackness could be achieved by avoiding the representation of interracial relationships. The counter-intuitiveness of the interracial in black queer texts is precisely what makes the representation of it so complex. Another way to understand what is happening with interraciality in these black queer texts is to think about them as counter-discourses that signify on the ideas embodied by the rhetoric they resist. Counter-discourses always rely upon the ideology they contest. As Michelle Wright demonstrates in her book *Becoming Black* (2004), in the context of her argument, counter-discursive arguments are characterized by an inability to "wholly segregate Black and white intellectual traditions in the West from one another."[15] We can apply this same logic to black queer counter-discursive representations of interraciality. Given black nationalism's own preoccupation with rejecting the interracial, it should not be surprising, then, that some texts by black queer artists would use nationalist tropes to subvert its claims about same-sex desire.[16] The black queer artists I discuss here put this racial mechanism to work for themselves in order to contest the construction that to be queer is to be something other than "black." By doing so they at once participate in one of the oldest and most traditional conventions in African American literature and also taunt the sensibilities of the black nationalist.

In all the texts I analyze, an interracial experience functions to stage blackness for the protagonists. In some texts, racial essentialism is disavowed and the interracial relationship operates in positive ways; others stage the interracial relationship, critique it, and then reject it. In this sense, most of the texts rework black nationalism to reveal the black queer subject's presence within the nation. In some cases that "new" vision of the black nation is one that renders it untenable. Not all of these narratives suggest that the black nation can be rescued or even untangled from whiteness. But they are all in dialogue with black nationalism about the place of the black queer subject in the nation. The device of interraciality, which highlights the race of its participants, also indicates that blackness has never been a stable and unchanging category. Rather, the interracial demonstrates that blackness operates as "a consciousness as well as a condition."[17] Therefore, these authors use interraciality as a trope to deconstruct and reconstruct the black nation as they see fit. One aspect of my argument here is that black queers are always already black and have never "left" the community. The interracial narrative operates to counter-discursively contest the nationalist discourses which attempted to excommunicate the black queer from the nation. And the use of the interracial narrative, as I show in this introduction, is a long-standing tradition in African American letters.

## Miscegephors

By discussing the gap between Marlon Riggs's choice of a life partner and the dénouement to his film, I am moving toward a question about the function of the interracial in the black queer text rather than attempting to expose Riggs as a hypocrite. What interests me about this disjunction is not what it can or cannot reveal about Riggs, but what it exposes about the deployment of the interracial as a trope. It seems to me that the representation of interraciality in texts is often treated in sociological terms—as if something "real" were at stake. Rather than see interraciality as a conceit, as a device, as a metaphor, we see it as something that actually exists. My examination of the interracial in these texts beseeches the reader to begin thinking about miscegenation and/or interraciality in the same way one would think about representations of "the mammy" or "the sambo"—that is, as a thing standing in for an idea rather than as a fact. So instead of using the familiar word "miscegenation," I have coined the term "miscegephors," to make present the notion that we are already talking about a symbolic, rather than an actual, act—a point I make below.

One of the things that struck me as I encountered some of the most important black queer texts was the prevalence of the interracial theme. In addition to the texts I consider here, there are other significant texts of the black queer canon, such as Audre Lorde's *Zami: A New Spelling of My Name* (1982), Melvin Dixon's *Vanishing Rooms* (2001), Darieck Scott's *Traitor to the Race* (1995), James Baldwin's *Giovanni's Room*[18] (1956), and Ruth Ellis's *Living with Pride @ 100* (1999), that represent interracial desire.[19] Critically speaking, questions of interracial,

same-sex desire have preoccupied many black theorists, among them
Dwight McBride, E. Patrick Johnson, Marlon B. Ross, Robert Reid-
Pharr, Darieck Scott, Christopher Cutrone, Guy Mark Foster, Jewelle
Gomez, Frantz Fanon, and Phillip Brian Harper, to name just a few.
That ideologies of race and sexuality are ideological bedfellows is the
premise of much valuable work on the subject. Examining this perpetually consummated union has preoccupied a range of brilliant scholars,
from Sander Gilman to Siobhan Somerville to José Muñoz.[20] One of the
ways the coupling of the interracial and/or miscegenation and homosexuality (in particular) has been explained is through the interrogation of eugenics discourses. The most notable critiques of the eugenic
pairing of miscegenation and homosexuality come from Somerville,
whose work interrogates representations of mulattos, miscegenation,
and homosexuality. The central assertion of this line of critique is
that theories of race and sexuality function as mutually constitutive
discourses, thereby creating each other through the language of the
"science" of reproduction, nationalism, and various forms of juridi-
cal surveillance (like the one-drop rule, or the law of hypodescent).
The so-called scientific logic of eugenics gave rise to the notion that
miscegenation would result in the production of an amalgamated third
subject, i.e., the mulatto or mixed-race person.

Eugenics figured miscegenation as something that happened *between*
and *to* bodies. And the status of the mixed-race individual in society,
according to eugenics, could be correlated entirely to the body. Indeed,
eugenicists perceived the mixed-race body as trapped in a perpetual
civil war of the self, as the "opposites" it contained agitated against
each other and undermined the unity of its subject. Homosexuality was
understood in much the same way—as a condition that could be read
upon the body, as a failure of physical sexual formation.[21] Hence miscegenation and homosexuality are characterized as similarly disabled
bodies, being weak and flawed, and ultimately harmful to the nation.
That harm is evidenced by the fact that neither miscegenation nor
homosexuality produces the racially homogeneous subjects the nation
imagines it needs to perpetuate the myth of its purity. Somerville and
others examine the anxiety around these issues in a series of texts. What
I am getting at here is that black queer artists are not the only artists
who produce texts which represent same-sex desire and interraciality.
In fact, we could historicize these texts along a continuum with texts

outside of the black queer canon.[22] Our analysis of the ways in which black queer artists represent interraciality and same-sex desire, however, must proceed from the knowledge that there are different things at stake in black representations. What is happening in black texts is quite different from the problematic eugenic politics which characterize the texts and contexts discussed in the work of the previously mentioned critics. While black queer texts "disidentify"[23] and signify on the apprehensions in the larger culture around miscegenation and same-sex desire, black queer texts subvert the biological and "scientific" logic of eugenics. Instead of attempting to ground questions of racial and sexual identity in the physical, black queer texts directly and metaphorically refigure racial and sexual identity in order to contest homophobic rhetoric from within the black community.

Miscegenation is, of course, a state of mind. If it is true that race is a social construction, and indeed it is, miscegenation is something that happens in the frontal lobe—not something that happens between bodies. Hence, it occurs not so much *between* bodies as *within* them. Identifying miscegenation as an interior operation, rather than a description of an external act, permits the realization that miscegenation is always a metaphor and never a(n) (f)act. The recognition of the negotiable nature of miscegenation as a symbol, a metaphor, and a trope is one way to understand the use of it as a device in black literature. The presumed deracinating power of miscegenation is not performed; rather, it is used to stage questions about race, authenticity, and belonging. This is the most consistent difference between black queer texts which couple interraciality and same-sex desire, and white representations of the same.[24] It is important to note that my argument is not about phenotype or visual economies. It isn't that the black queer subject only sees herself as more authentically black because of her "visual" relationship to the white queer other. I am tempted to say that my argument is not about actual bodies, but that isn't the most precise statement. It might be more accurate to say that the interracial narrative can be understood as mapping a set of ideas about bodies, where the power of the racialized thought bears more representational weight than actual flesh does.

The interracial demarcates and tests the boundaries of race. One view of what interraciality does is that it blurs the categories of "x" race and "y" race, so that there is a "blending" of the two. This idea has been both the fear and the hope of all kinds of people on either side of the issue.[25] I argue, however, that miscegenation does not contribute to a blending of any kind, but rather reifies the notion of disparate racial identity. As the subject thinks about miscegenation, she confronts the perceived racial difference of the interracial couple. Therefore each reference to, or reminder of, miscegenation is always an allusion to the idea of racial purity. Hence miscegenation does not blur racial boundaries, but rigidifies them. The use of miscegenation as a metaphor, which stresses one's racial position rather than undermines it, is one important aspect of black signifying on the interracial site. This contradicts the logic which argues, especially in a black context, that to choose a white lover is to disavow and repudiate one's blackness. In most of these black queer texts, one way the device of the interracial functions to rigidify racial identity is to stage the failure of the interracial relationship, which dramatizes the black subject's location within blackness.

The liberal vision of the interracial relationship imagines that by coming together, black and white people can transcend the ugliness of racism. Growing up as a biracial child in a household with a black mother and a white father (and, later, a white stepfather), race was never far from my mind. In my earliest imaginings about what it meant to be "half black and half white," I wondered if that meant I was kind of like a black and white checkerboard or if I could be bisected, with one whole white side and one whole black side. I never was more aware of both of my parents' race as when my stepfather asked my mother if he could borrow her makeup because he was going to act the part of "night" in a play. As a dark-skinned Italian, my stepfather was not as white as he imagined himself, though in his mind, my mother was as black as Al Jolson on a Saturday night. We can also see how race takes center stage in Darieck Scott's novel *Traitor to the Race*. The racially motivated death of his cousin sparks a crisis in the protagonist's relationship with his white partner, which argues against the notion of the interracial relationship as the site of racial forgetting.[26] This isn't to say that the interracial isn't instructive and perhaps even generative, but it does indicate that the idea that cross-racial romance undermines one's racial identity is at best only a partial picture of what it means to love someone whose racial identity differs from one's own.

We see the racinating possibility of the interracial fantasy in Frantz Fanon's formulation of miscegenation in *Black Skin, White Masks*

(1952). Even as Fanon triangulates his desire for white women through his desire to become a white man, his blackness comes into vivid focus: "Out of the blackest part of my soul . . . surges this desire to be suddenly white."[27] And later he notes, "A coal-black Negro, in a Paris bed with a 'maddening blonde,' shouted at the moment of orgasm, 'Hurrah for Schoelcher!'"[28] In this passage blackness is emphasized. Notice that this miscegenated desire comes from the *blackest* part of himself, that the Negro in the bed with the blonde is *coal-black*. In the miscegenation fantasy, all Negroes are coal-black because miscegenation is not about racial indeterminacy or fluidity. It is imagined in extremity: the blonde and the (coal) black. Whether the woman in the fantasy is *really* a tawny Italian with a peroxide job and the man a light-skinned Ethiopian, the miscegenation fantasy is one where they are only, and can only ever be, "black" and "blonde" (read: white). Fanon's description of the people involved here is imaginary; no other bodily "reality" can supersede the projection of difference the interracial fantasy involves. Miscegenation does not efface blackness despite the ostensible desire for whiteness. Instead it highlights blackness, making it visible in the "zebra striping," to use Fanon's term, of the (black) mind. But the bodies of these people are no more "black" and "white" than Fanon's mind is zebra striped because the racialized body is always *imagined* as such.

We can also see how blackness functions in the interracial context in Dwight McBride's essay "It's a White Man's World: Race in the Gay Marketplace of Desire." Writing about a sexual encounter with a white flight attendant, McBride clearly performs his blackness by relating an experience with racism right after they have sex:

> When it was over and we had talked for a while, I made ready to leave to go home . . . He smiled at me as I was getting dressed to leave and said, "Congratulations." I was caught off guard by this declaration. I said, "I'm sorry?" He repeated, "Congratulations," still smiling. "For what?" I asked. "You're the first black guy I've ever let do what we just did," he said, fully satisfied with the sufficiency of his response. I dressed more quickly now.[29]

McBride's experience with the flight attendant inscribes him as a black subject because immediately following sex, he is named as "black" by his partner and also imbued with some "special" status since he popped the young man's racial cherry, so to speak. What we can see in both McBride's and Fanon's experience of the interracial is an attention to and reaffirmation of black identity. Contrary to liberal notions of the interracial, where race is elided and transcended, the interracial functions as ground zero for highlighting race, though according to Christopher Cutrone, interracial intimacy is potentially utopic *because* it makes race visible.[30] What we can learn from Fanon's performance of this phenotypic opposition of blackness and whiteness is that miscegenation is not a sex act, but an *idea* about sex. It is a fantasy that frames bodies, and hence desire, but it—like the racial categories it seeks to eroticize—does not exist as more than a construction.

From its inception, African American literature has been rich with miscegephors. In fact, it is arguable that almost the entire canon of African American literature, at least until the Black Arts Movement, is preoccupied with questions of intermixing, passing, miscegenation, and mixed-race identity (though it isn't often called such). From the first novel ever written by an African American, William Wells Brown's *Clotel* (1853), to Charles Chestnutt's *House behind the Cedars* (1900), to Frances Harper's *Iola Leroy* (1892), to *Plum Bun* (1929), the novels of Nella Larsen, to Sutton Griggs's *Imperium en Imperio* (1899), to W. E. B. Du Bois's *The Dark Princess* (1928), to *The Autobiography of an Ex-Colored Man* (1912), to *The Blacker The Berry* (1929)—the themes of racial intermixture and miscegenation are incredibly prevalent in African American literature. Typically miscegenation has been represented as taboo in African American culture. This is undoubtedly due to the fact that miscegenation was illegal until 1967, and evidence of racial mixture between blacks and whites was marked by histories of violence and slavery. In most of the aforementioned texts, miscegenation is represented quite frequently through the passing figure, or the miscegenated figure, who we might read as standing in for questions raised about sex and blood "mixing" which any discussion of miscegenation inevitably concerns.

Yet the passing figure poses a different set of questions in the African American context than in the white one. This is because the discursive history of racial purity and threat structure blackness and whiteness differently. For example, M. Giulia Fabi notes:

> Although scholars have often taken for granted and overestimated their similarity, white-authored representations of the tragic mulatto and *African American representations of miscegenation and*

*passing constitute profoundly different literary traditions.* Of course, this does not mean that they do not share common elements, but shared and inherited elements do crystallize in unique literary configurations. For instance, in pre–Harlem Renaissance African American fiction the passers are rarely tragic figures, and even when tragedy does befall them, it is most clearly indicated to be the result of virulent prejudice and discrimination. The lingering suspicion that the mulatto's or mulatta's downfall may stem from some intrinsic, genetic flaw of character is conspicuously absent. (emphasis added)[31]

So while the passing figure in some contexts destabilizes whiteness, the passing figure also expands our conception of blackness. Put another way, we might see the passing figure and the miscegenation narrative not only as dramatizing racial threat to whiteness, but also as devices for reimagining blackness. Hazel Carby has noted the use of passing as a narrative device, writing that the passing figure is a "vehicle for an exploration of the relationship between the races."[32] Yet the passing figure not only highlights interracial issues, it also focuses on intraracial concerns—specifically the articulation of an "authentically" black identity, as critics like Valerie Smith and Gayle Walde argue.[33] This paradigm shift happens when we move the site of our inquiry from whiteness to blackness. This revision occurs when the boundary between the passing/mixed-race figure and the black figure is collapsed. How might we understand the way black bodies function as the universal body, since *all bodies* can be black bodies? By this I mean that bodies which we think of as "white," bodies which we think of as "black," even bodies we think of as appearing to be Latino or "Asian" can all be "black bodies."[34] Hypodescent is not the only structure in the context of the black community that defines who is black. Part of what is operating here, as well, is a tacit knowledge that race is always already constructed. Hence the black community defined itself in ways that transcended and contested the bodily logic of racism. Unlike Naomi Zack, who argues that during the Harlem Renaissance the mixed-race individual functioned as a "theoretical wedge against"[35] race thought, I am arguing, as Robert Reid-Pharr does in another context,[36] that the collapsing of the distinction between the mulatto/passing figure and the black person *in the context of the black community* redefined blackness itself. One site where this negotiation of blackness takes place is in the passing narrative. For a black readership, the passing narrative works to claim "white" bodies as black and hence the boundaries of blackness expand to include any and all bodies, regardless of phenotype. Brown is black is yellow is black is white is black, but white, in the context of white identity, is only white. This reliance on the false empiricism of the body—for even as race is proclaimed a social construction, that construction is most often deployed to deconstruct the person of color's status as other—structures miscegenation differently in black and white contexts. In the context of white identity, miscegenation can only undo. In the context of black identity, miscegenation creates.[37]

So what is blackness then if not, primarily, a set of easily identifiable and definable bodies? This is the central question of African American letters, and there is no definitive answer (nor should there be). My first impulse is to celebrate the way any examination of blackness demonstrates that the stunning revelation of race as a social construction is one that seems to underlie African American thinking since at least 1903.[38] This enthusiasm is a little checked, though, by the knowledge that though a social construction, race has often been deployed in very real and problematic ways, and the black community is not immune from troubling and exclusive definitions of race. Yet the mutability of blackness, and the tools that are used by black artists to remake it and revise it, abides as a defining factor of black artistic production. Michelle Wright notes that blackness is a constantly changing construct: "Black subjectivity . . . is defined not by a common history or a common cultural trope but by a particular theoretical *methodology*."[39] (I would also add that blackness is not defined by a common *body*.) Invoking miscegenation through the trope of the interracial is one such methodology used to underscore black subjectivity. Therefore we can understand interraciality as a metaphor which works to consolidate black identity rather than compromise it, exposing the black subject's location *within* blackness. These miscegephors counter-discursively solidify and bring blackness—perhaps a reimagined blackness—into focus.

Interraciality invokes a historical narrative about the constant renegotiation of blackness throughout the history of the United States. Werner Sollors suggests that the miscegenation narrative is a distinctively *American* mode of thinking through the nation.[40] It is no coincidence that the first novel written by an African American, William

Wells Brown's *Clotel* (1853), is a "miscegenated" tale preoccupied with the most intimate (and unmentionable) questions of American nationalism.[41] Changing notions of black identity have often been staged at the site of miscegenation or around "mulatto" identity; hence the use of miscegenation and/or the interracial as a textual device suggests that a remaking of race is under way in the text that employs it. To invoke the trope of interracial sex, then, is to allude to other moments in black textual history that considered the mulatto and miscegenation—all of which moments are characterized by a shift in black thought about blackness itself. For example, the Harlem Renaissance was one such moment when literary representations of miscegenation and the mulatto proliferated. Yet the Harlem Renaissance is also seen as moment when, as Robert Reid-Pharr notes, "the production of modern American notions of racial distinctiveness rigidified."[42] In the introductory essay to *The New Negro* (1925), Alain Locke characterizes the change in the African American population as a "new psychology."[43] He notes that the "New Negro" arises from a "common consciousness" rather than a "common condition" among African Americans.[44] Locke clearly identifies the creation of a "new" black identity as transcending "condition," which can be read as including color, along with other significant factors like class. Instead he locates blackness at the site of the psychological, as a consciousness rather than as a state of physical being. Blackness, he asserts, is more a state of mind than a state of body. In so doing, he marks the Harlem Renaissance as a moment when the process of reimagining the black subject occurs methodologically and ideologically.

This revision of the black subject during the Harlem Renaissance coincided with the popularity of the passing narrative during the period, and concerns about passing and miscegenation reached a climax. As I have already noted, texts that interrogate the passing figure and interracial desire predate the Harlem Renaissance and characterize African American writing from its very inception. The concurrence of narratives of passing/miscegenation and the renegotiation of black identity demonstrates that miscegenation activates particular narratives about the discursive nature of "blackness." In this way, the writers and thinkers of the Harlem Renaissance were participating in a literary tradition of testing the boundaries of blackness through the miscegenation narrative, redrawing borders and illuminating racial fault lines. To put it another way, the topoi of miscegenation has historically signaled the rethinking of racial identity. If it is true, as Eva Saks argues, that miscegenation laws helped "create and enforce"[45] race as a metaphor, it stands to reason that the textual manipulation of it can have significant impact on how we think about race and racial identity. In other words, by invoking the interracial, black artists recreate our conception of blackness.

## Revolutionary Acts

If we understand "queer" to describe "things that can't be made to line up neatly,"[46] then the play between representation and reality, between the personal and the political, is the queer moment. The contradictions between Marlon Riggs's autobiography and his life reveal that the last word might not be the last word. What can we make of Riggs's final statement, quoted as the epigraph at the beginning of this introduction, and his commitment to Jack, his white life partner? Perhaps there is nothing to make of this; we could separate the two, reading one as text, and the other as life, and hence off-limits. Yet given the autobiographical nature of the film *Tongues Untied,* it is worth considering what is at stake in the film's final proclamation.

As I write this I am struck by how irrelevant it feels to me, on one level, to interrogate the question. I don't care at all about the contradiction; it does not discredit Riggs or the spirit of his work. It does not reveal anything disingenuous about either "text." Nor does his partner Jack invalidate the claim made at the end of the film; rather, it exposes the narrative interdependency of black/white and black/black couplings. For it is the movement from a paradigm of the black/white interracial to the black/black intraracial that enables the film's ultimate claim. It is worth noting that this is a quotation, so the final statement represents a collective, rather than an individual, voice. The entire film, in fact, moves from individual, personal isolation, to multiplicity, to community. Yet the "text" of Riggs's lifelong relationship with a white man and the text of the film work *together* to perform the black queer's place in the black nation. I am struck by the ideological similarity between Joseph Beam's statement and one of the oft-quoted bromides of the 1960s: "Black is Beautiful." Black nationalism aims to inculcate in blacks love for each other, to put one's "brother" above all outsiders. Riggs takes this idea of "brotherly love" and turns it on its head, exploiting the erotic possibilities within that nationalist configuration.

Black *is* beautiful, but that doesn't mean white is ugly. The opposite formulation which the platitude "black is beautiful" contests is "black is ugly." I bring this up here because a similar unpacking of "Black men loving Black men is *THE* revolutionary act" might not be "Black men loving White men is *THE* counterrevolutionary act," but rather "Black men hating Black men is *THE* counterrevolutionary act!" Riggs frames the film's statement about the nature of "revolutionary" desire by critiquing the interracial when it suppresses love between black men. Hence, Riggs sets his desire for his *first* white lover against the backdrop of homophobia. Riggs traces his becoming a "snow queen" to a white man who helps him after an attack by homophobes. He marks this as problematic by indicating that his desire for whiteness equaled, for him, a repudiation of blackness. He says that he would not meet the eyes of another gay black man on the street because he sought only "white flesh." This opposition, of desire for whiteness and repudiation of the black self, structures the film's interrogation of the interracial. It is this apparently contrary avowal of interracial desire that effectively grounds Riggs in blackness. In his indication that he wouldn't meet the eyes of another black gay man, Riggs implicitly suggests that he *should* meet the eyes of a black gay man. By turning away, he highlights that about himself which he refuses to confront. Through the act of looking for white flesh, Riggs becomes aware of himself, as a black man, *not-looking* for black flesh. Put another way, interraciality shows blackness to itself.

The schism between Riggs and the black community that the beginning of the film documents is undone by a symbolic return to blackness. Stylistically, Riggs unifies the black community and the black gay community through the use of dance. *Tongues Untied* ends with several dance segments. The first is a vogueing sequence, which fades into actors doing the electric slide, a dance particular to African American culture.[47] The electric slide works in *Tongues Untied* as a cultural signifier in the same way that the film uses vogueing to signify something specifically "black" and "gay." Significantly, the electric slide is both communal and culturally specific. It is a group dance, and it highlights participation rather than performance. Like vogueing, it is dependent on a collective and functions to affirm group connections.

The voiceover during the electric slide tells us, "Ironic that dance, my ticket to assimilation, my way of amusing and then winning acceptance —that the same steps were now my passage back home." Interwoven in this scene is a transposed black-and-white image of a young black boy dancing a shuffle for a crowd of white onlookers. The image is grainy and its quality and style of photography suggest that it is an old recording, alluding to the notion of black people as valuable only when entertaining white people, particularly as dancers. In *American Notes* (1842), Charles Dickens observes a black man, William Henry Lane, dancing in New York and describes it in great detail. His description of Lane is important because, as Maurice Wallace notes in his discussion of it, this moment has "historically coalesced to shape black masculine subjecthood in Eurocentric contexts."[48] Introducing this related image during the electric slide sequence references dance as a means for black men to manage (as Riggs notes in his voiceover) their exclusion and vilification in American society.

*Tongues Untied* reconceptualizes dance in relation to black masculinity, using it to symbolically connect two communities that the film has constructed—up to this point—as separate. Dance as a signifier, then, is one that brings into coherence issues of gay and black identity in this film (through vogueing and then the electric slide) in a way that few signifiers do as effectively. The fade from vogueing, associated primarily with an ethnic gay culture, to the electric slide, associated with the black community, layered on top of the history of black people dancing for a white audience, is a significant stylistic illustration of the film's closing statement. Riggs accomplishes this by superimposing the images of the electric slide over that of the little boy dancing after the fade from the vogueing sequence. This layering of images breaks down the discursive oppositions which initially structured black and gay identity. In this way, Riggs collapses the boundary between "black" and "gay" and shows the black nation, in all its complexity, to itself.

## On Loyalty

*Who's to say that dating someone white doesn't make me black?*

—Cheryl, *The Watermelon Woman*

Regardless of my intention to locate the black queer subject in relation to blackness, even in the interracial narrative, some readers will undoubtedly ask the question: Why do black queer artists *need* to employ miscegenation or interraciality in their work? The short answer to that question is that black queer artists don't *need* to address interraciality in their work at all. But the fact is many of them do. It is also true that many of them don't. There are representations of black queer identity in many cultural, ethnic, and classed contexts; some of those contexts are monoracial, or all black.[49] Those texts are no less important or valid than the texts I discuss here. But quite a few of the texts which inaugurate a genre (for instance, the first black same-sex novel or film or album) do indeed comment on, stage, and enact interracial desire.

In my attention to the interracial, I follow the narrative trajectory *of the works themselves;* and I consider these particular works because of their significance to the black queer canon. Because black national-ism traditionally mobilized to exclude gay and lesbian subjects from the nation by accusing them of colluding with whiteness, some cringe at the thought of even calling attention to the ways in which black queer discourse represents the interracial. There is an understandable fear that attention to the interracial will buttress claims that to be black and gay is to betray the race and to be "less authentically black." *Queer in Black and White* contests this notion that the black queer subject is not "black enough," and accounts for the frequent representation of the interracial as a device used to signify on the idea of the nation, of authenticity, and of blackness. But by paying so much attention to the representation of interraciality, I trigger the impulse to disavow these "problematic" representations of interracial desire.

As I have already pointed out, the representation of interracial desire is a striking aspect of black queer signifying, from the works of James Baldwin, to Cheryl Dunye, to Audre Lorde, to Ann Allen Shockley, to Marlon Riggs and many others. Yet, to speak about interracial desire is, astonishingly, still a risk. Writing about Robert Reid-Pharr's frank discussion of his white lover Rick in *Black Gay Man,* Dwight McBride says, "At the same time that something lodged deep inside me reviled him in this moment, I also revered his courage to speak so candidly and eloquently from experience about the complications that animate our sexual and intimate lives."[50] McBride at once "reviles" Reid-Pharr and identifies his "outing" of himself as a lover of a white man as cou-rageous. Both feelings indicate that to write about interracial desire, especially in the black context, and specifically to write about desiring a white person, carries with it tremendous danger. Indeed, McBride goes on to share his own experience with a white lover, a scene which I analyze earlier, but he sets up his sharing of the details of his own interracial intimacy through the tentative language of fear. He writes, "I am afraid of the ramifications . . . I am afraid that people will not understand."[51] It feels astonishingly dangerous to me to suggest that this fear McBride talks about is the mark of how far we have *not* come. It is a sign that interracial desire still operates pathologically in our collective imagination and this, of course, is not progress.

But as Reid-Pharr points out in his introduction to *Black Gay Man,* after he shares the very information which prompts revulsion, and admiration, in McBride, "I believe that the image of Rick continues to be disruptive only insofar as one continues to support the false assumption that political identity is always the ultimate result of rational decision making and never a question of aesthetics, an act of self-pleasuring."[52] Within Reid-Pharr's analysis is the suggestion that loving the white other can be generative, i.e., self-pleasuring, to the black self. That cross-racial desire does not undermine but can actually please, if you will, the black self is one of the points I am trying to make in *Queer in Black and White*. This is the idea behind the epigraph to this section. As Cheryl asks in *The Watermelon Woman,* who says loving a white person doesn't make one black? This reversal explicitly rejects the nationalist script that formulates interracial desire as deracinating.

Simply ignoring the fact that black queer signifying has staged and confronted questions of interracial desire, and continues to do so, cannot destabilize homophobic claims about racial authenticity. I fear, not unlike McBride, that some readers of this book will not understand what is truly at stake in my examination of the interracial. By examining in close detail the function of the interracial in these important texts by gay, lesbian, and bisexual African American artists, *Queer in Black and White* argues for a reading of those texts that renders them firmly within the African American tradition, where blackness is asserted rather than undermined. I am arguing that the interracial "*reracinates*" the black queer subject,[53] hence rejecting the nationalist and homophobic logic which excludes the black gay and lesbian subject from blackness. At the same time, I do not mean to suggest that blackness *should* be reified as an uncontested site of belonging. I, too, "shudder at the thought of offering yet another rescripting of black identity that turns on the celebration of a never quite attainable, wholly sanitized, black normativity,"[54] but articulating what is at stake in many of the texts I examine requires an attention to blackness and to the claims, most specifically in relation to sexuality, which define black identity.

# "IRONIC SOIL"

## RECUPERATIVE RHYTHMS AND NEGOTIATED NATIONALISMS

*The fact of the matter is that major nationalist theoreticians have generally been exceedingly humanistic . . . In fact, a strong tendency to reach beyond themselves toward union with mankind has been a marked characteristic of most nationalist theoreticians from David Walker to Paul Robeson. The nationalists' concern for their fellow man should be kept in mind in order to avoid doing violence to the meaning of historic black nationalism.*

—Sterling Stuckey

*I worry at this particular moment in our history where a lot of the gains that were brought about, to a certain extent, by some of the more positive attributes of nationalism are really being threatened. As much as I would like to eliminate the radically exclusionary attitudes of certain forms of black nationalism, I don't want to get rid of Affirmative Action and I really feel strongly about making these distinctions.*

—Coco Fusco

In "It's Raining Men: Notes on the Million Man March," Robert Reid-Pharr eloquently describes the difficulty of relating black nationalist discourse to homosexuality. This difficulty is founded on the assumption that blackness and homosexuality are mutually exclusive, that gay, lesbian, and bisexual people are the nation's antagonists.[1] This notion that blackness and heterosexuality are natural pairs and that "authentic" blackness cannot contain or does not include queer identifications as well is one that has been aptly and frequently deconstructed and commented on by critics such as Phillip Brian Harper, Audre Lorde, Wahneema Lubiano, Dwight McBride, Rhonda M. Williams, E. Patrick Johnson, Kendall Thomas, and others.[2] Reid-Pharr identifies the blatant homophobia embodied in the rhetoric of the Million Man March, noting that "if the real message of the march was that it is going to take a heroic black masculinity to restore order to our various communities, especially poor and working-class communities, then it follows that black gay men are irrelevant, or even dangerous, to that project."[3] Reid-Pharr aptly distinguishes the politics of the "nation" (and here, the black nation largely writ could be said to have been collapsed under the sign of the "Nation" of Islam since Louis Farrakhan was the instigator of the march) as embodied by the march as black, as heterosexual, and as exclusive of women. Like the aforementioned critiques of black nationalism, which is invested in a disciplining and policing of sexuality and gender, Reid-Pharr identifies the politics of the march as bound to the same homophobic and sexist logic that has often been an undeniable aspect of black nationalism. Reid-Pharr notes, "For, if the definition of blackness hinges on heterosexuality, then either blackness and homosexuality are incommensurable (and black gays are not really black) or the notion of blackness is untenable, as witnessed by the large numbers of black gay men."[4]

Of course, as Reid-Pharr goes on to note immediately after this passage, contemporary gay and lesbian thought makes the previous quoted possibility an impossibility. Advancing the notion that essentialist notions of blackness exclude the possibility of homosexuality is, I am attempting to point out here, a necessarily much discussed aspect of the study of race and sexuality. However, what I seek to examine is the way a critique of black nationalism does not necessarily move one past the nationalist moment. Indeed, what I discuss herein is a queering of black nationalism that stretches and bends the limits of nationalism so that it can include those identities and subjects it views as outlaw. I begin with the invocation of Reid-Pharr's essay because though he thoroughly and ably unpacks the problematic aspects of the Million Man March's rhetoric, he ends by noting, "Here, then, despite the regressive racial and gender politics that framed the Million Man March, there were countless improvisational moments of transcendence."[5] Reid-Pharr's consideration of the Million Man March, then, is not at all a dismissal of the event based on its predictably anachronistic political implications. Rather, Reid-Pharr's essay participates in an emerging trend at queer sites that not only calls black nationalism's heterosexism into question, but also, and perhaps most importantly, seeks to invade it, to subvert it and deconstruct the logic of nationalism by occupying its space. These renegotiations of nationalism traverse the boundary of the "almost not quite" that opens a previously closed space for once-excluded identities. The focus of this chapter is on the emergence of such "improvisational moments of transcendence" in queer discourses that remake, renegotiate, and revamp nationalism.

Despite the critique of nationalism delineated above, it is clear that for many critics, like Coco Fusco and Sterling Stuckey, whose words are quoted in this chapter's epigraphs, black nationalism cannot be dismissed. This unwillingness to dismiss black nationalism is due, in large part, to the persistence of racism; in a country horribly scarred by the tragedies of race it is understandable that a discourse and rhetoric which figure themselves as overturning and opposing racism would continue to be relevant for African Americans. It is no doubt because of this racism that in same-sex discourses "race emerges unscathed. Indeed, blackness has been bolstered, insofar as we were all forced [at the Million Man March and, as I argue here, at other "black" sites], at least those of us who are black *and* otherwise, to scurry for cover under the great black mantle, to fly our colors."[6] Black nationalism's appeal, which is irremovable from its problematic, then, is rooted in a complicated set of needs and aversions. Let us focus briefly on the need it serves. In his seminal essay for *The Ideological Origins of Black Nationalism,* Sterling Stuckey defines black nationalism in this way:

> A consciousness of a shared experience of oppression at the hands of white people, an awareness and approval of the persistence of group traits and preferences in spite of a violently anti-African larger society, a recognition of bonds and obligations between Africans everywhere, an irreducible conviction that Africans in America must take responsibility for liberating themselves—these were among the pivotal components of the world view of the black men who finally framed the ideology.[7]

This "consciousness of a shared experience of oppression" is the pivotal component that continues to exist today. The shared experience of oppression is an "everyday" reality in the lives of most people defined as "black" by American society. The latter part of this quote by Stuckey speaks to what Wahneema Lubiano, in her essay "Black Nationalism and Black Common Sense: Policing Ourselves and Others," calls "everyday ideology." That black people must "liberate themselves," as Stuckey says, is the cornerstone of this everyday ideology, which Lubiano defines as "the cultural logic of black peoples' historical self-consciousness."[8] This cultural logic is what dictates the feeling of anger at "black on black crime" within the black community. Essex Hemphill exemplifies this sentiment in a poem: "Black men killing black men is treason. Black men killing black women is treason."[9] The reliance here on a black nationalist logic is indicated by the use of the word "treason," which by definition indicates a betrayal of the state. It is the same logic that encourages one to "buy black" in order to support African American economic growth and development.[10] All of these issues and concerns are part of what Coco Fusco might call the more "positive attributes of nationalism."[11]

As Coco Fusco hints, however, nationalist loyalties also have negative attributes. Stuckey's definition of black nationalism, for example, excludes women in a mimesis of Eurocentric nationalist notions of "forefathers" as the founders of a liberating ideology. There is also the uninterrogated term "blackness," which does not account for "the shifting multiplicities of a group that understands itself as 'black.'"[12] Furthermore, as others have argued elsewhere, as noted above, nationalism is also deeply interested in the reproduction of the nation through heterosexuality. In this chapter I discuss a text that manages a negotiation of black nationalism which at once internalizes some problematic nationalist notions while at the same time subverts nationalist logic to allow for queer identities. I want to focus on one site in black gay and lesbian production that "represent[s] black gays and lesbians as integral, if beleaguered, members of the black family,"[13] and especially on how this membership in the family of blackness is achieved. I want not only to demonstrate the difficulties such nationalist paradigms pose, but also to consider why they continue to be entertained, what they accomplish, for what means and by whom.

While ultimately I would argue that there is no way to "fix" nationalism so that it will work, I want to consider texts that negotiate nationalism in interesting and, even if only in a limited sense, productive ways. As Lubiano points out, "black nationalism is plural, flexible and contested,"[14] which means that it expands to legitimate certain forms of desire and to exclude others. One reason for discussing texts that recuperate nationalism in some way is to give serious attention to an ideology that continues to be important to articulations of black subjectivity. Despite intense skepticism and scrutiny, it remains true that black nationalism is "extremely complicated, often reactionary, and dangerously effective in the way that it can and has organized specific groups of black people, under specific circumstances."[15] In other words, despite its shortcomings—and because of them—it deserves our attention. This seems especially significant at a moment when the landscape of political mobilization has shifted so radically and so quickly that the articulation of a "black" response to national crises that affect the African American community has become increasingly difficult to negotiate; the Million Man March is just one example of the way our shifting and multiple constituencies within the black community complicate our "nation." Alluding again to the epigraph of Coco Fusco, we can see that the question of nationalism as activism is one that remains relevant in the black community. This essay explores one such site of negotiated nationalism, an early 1990s reconsideration of nationalism by a subject that nationalism, as it has been traditionally conceptualized, would normally seek to exclude.

The album *Plantation Lullabies* (1993), by Me'Shell NdegéOcello, is a good example of the kind of recuperative rhythms and negotiated nationalisms I seek to discuss here. It is significant not only because of its musical content (the soundtrack) but also because of the photographs and artwork in the CD booklet (its visual track). With song titles like "Soul on Ice" and "Dread Loc," *Plantation Lullabies* articulates a form of nationalism that blends black militancy with Afrocentricity. This strain of nationalism is bracketed by the emergence of Kwanzaa and an ideological reliance on Egyptian and Yoruba religious traditions. For many of the proponents of this form of nationalism, such as Amen-Ra and Maulana Karenga, the goal was (and still is) to have black Americans return to an African tradition as "the first functional step toward a greater African American future."[16] For the moment I will define Afrocentricity as an approach that, as stated by Molefi Kete Asante, "seeks in every situation the appropriate centrality of the African person. In education this means that the teacher provides students the opportunity to study the world and its people, concepts, and history from an African world view."[17]

NdegéOcello's *Plantation Lullabies* voices anger at being deprived of this history: "We've been indoctrinated and convinced by the white racist standard of beauty," she tells us in "Soul on Ice," referencing Eldridge Cleaver's 1967 book of essays.[18] In this particular song, which alludes to Cleaver's discussion of black male desire for white women, NdegéOcello observes, "Your soul's on ice, brother. Brother, are you suffering from a social infection, mis-direction? Excuse me, does the white woman go better with your Brooks Brother suit?" And unlike Cleaver's version, NdegéOcello remembers to include the history of white men sexually exploiting black women: "But my, my! Master's been in the slave house again." This confrontation with racism is staged through antimiscegenation discourse and organizes NdegéOcello's political agenda on this album as specifically related to race. In 1993, however, when the album was released, these exclamations were not revolutionary.

These sentiments are little more than a rehearsal of black nationalist dogma as evidenced by the very text NdegéOcello references, *Soul on Ice*. One critic, in reviewing this album, wrote of this track: "'Soul On Ice' is probably her most controversial track. It's been a part of a very long-running thread in [African American culture]. Despite reports of her apparent okay-ness with interracial/cultural relationships, she seems to see no contradiction with also being annoyed with those who buy into 'the White racist standard of beauty.'"[19] What this reviewer misses is the possibility for multiple practices around interracial desire. NdegéOcello's calling out of the brother in the Brooks Brothers suit identifies a particular kind of subject, one that sees his white lover as an accoutrement to his class status. Likewise, her maligning of the white racist standard of beauty isn't the same thing as rejecting white love, or white people. Isn't it possible to love one's (black) self and also love a white person? Furthermore, what NdegéOcello's nationalist lyrics suggest is that her politics of "strengthening black community and reproducing the beauty of the 'race'"[20] are a complicated avowal of her own black body and all forms of desire she generates from within.

The same ethos of intraracial love which frames the proclamation in Marlon Riggs's *Tongues Untied* is evident on *Plantation Lullabies*. On the song "I'm Diggin' You (Like an Old Soul Record), NdegéOcello's nostalgia for the 1970s, when black nationalism was at its zenith, is evident when she sings, "Remember back in the day, when everyone was black and conscious and down for the struggle? Love brought us all together." She casts her memory in heterosexual terms: "Everything was cool and brothers were singing 'ain't no woman like the one I got.'" She then goes on to say that the only thing that can soothe her soul from drug use in the community and police brutality is "black-on-black love." This song suggests that "back then" there was an order that is now absent. Part of this fantasy is the ordering of relationships as heterosexual. Though NdegéOcello does not construct the threats to the black nation in homophobic terms, her reference to drugs and police brutality (and by extension to the incarceration of black men) is similar to what the women I discuss at the beginning of the introduction profess in *Jungle Fever* as the downfall of the black community. Along with her anti-interracial theme in the track "Soul on Ice," the songs on the album *Plantation Lullabies* articulate an incredibly conservative nationalist ideology.

The strong nationalist ideology continues on other tracks, even ones that seem at first to offer the possibility of a same-sex paradigm. On the song "untitled," she begins by describing a beautiful black woman, saying that this black woman's beauty cannot be measured by "colonized standards of beauty." While NdegéOcello directs our gaze in this song toward a beautiful black female body, the same-sex erotic possibilities are undercut by the end, when the song veers toward a male/female paradigm: "She cradles his body in her large hands . . . her caress warm and penetrating, she loves the black boy." She even goes so far as to cast this black male/female relationship as pure, ending by saying that "there's such purity in love that is essential to the loving of one's self." It is clear that black-on-black love is the only love that can be "pure," and that to love someone who is not black is to miss out on something essential, to miss out on self-love.

Along with this nationalist critique of miscegenation, NdegéOcello also performs heterosexuality most explicitly on the tracks "Dread Loc"—"ohh how I love a black man"—and on "Call Me," where she says, "I'll make you feel like a King, I'll be the Queen." The last example at once signifies on the rhetoric of Afrocentric discourses, which encourages African Americans to imagine a royal African lineage and past in order to salvage a self-esteem beaten down by oppression,[21] and at the same time, it plays on the king/queen rhetoric of gay subculture. The slippage between signifiers of black straight and gay/lesbian/bisexual subcultures is apparent in NdegéOcello's ambiguous lyrics here. But in the presumably heterosexual love songs on *Plantation Lullabies,* black masculinity and a pro-family rhetoric begin to emerge—which is not surprising since the album is so fully engaged with black nationalist discourse.

Like the material versus performative contradictions which mark the song "Soul on Ice," the heterosexual love songs on the album are complicated by NdegéOcello's professed bisexuality,[22] which is certainly a violation of black nationalist sexual politics, which are inherently and implicitly heterosexual. Despite the rehearsal of black nationalist racial and sexual ideologies, NdegéOcello's album manages to undercut these politics through its visual economy and through the discursive position NdegéOcello takes as the first-person singer in some of the other love songs, specifically "Outside Your Door" and "Picture Show." In both songs, NdegéOcello does not allude to black men but is tellingly silent as to the gender of the person she is wooing. We can read this as an open space in the sexual discourse which frames the album. Given the insistence on gendered identification in the songs discussed earlier, the silence in this regard on these other songs enables a same-sex reading. Adrienne Rich notes that "women's love for women has been represented almost entirely through silence and lies . . . Heterosexuality as an institution has also drowned in silence the erotic feelings between women."[23] However, NdegéOcello's desire for women is signaled (or represented, to use Rich's exact terminology) through silence and the "lie" of heterosexuality, which counterbalances the ambiguous gender of her object of desire on the other tracks. In other words, her album suggests that in order to be "down," she must subsume her sexual politics to her racial politics, a much-discussed problem in black nationalist discourses.[24] In those discourses, particularly masculine accounts of oppression take precedence over feminine ones, and black male heterosexual virility is a striking characteristic of the nationalist persona.[25] This tendency to elevate black nationalism (read here as specifically masculine desires and masculine concerns) to the exclusion of feminine discourses and/ or of same-sex discourses is a striking feature of this album.

But reading the album through a critical bisexuality opens up several readings across both its visual track and its soundtrack. If we understand bisexuality to be an "intersubjective matrix—a nonspecific but gendered, sexualized space where new modes of identity can occur,"[26] then our analysis can contain the contradictions of *Plantation Lullabies* as well as accommodate its slippery racial and sexual politics. NdegéOcello, as Mark Anthony Neal points out,

> never felt a need to defend or explain the supposed ambiguity that is so crucial to her music, because the "spaces and places" that she claims and cultivates are never in competition with themselves, but rather an admittedly complex and creative articulation of what it means to be "blackwomanbisexualbassplayersentientbeing Gramscianintellecualandrevolutionarysoulsinger." As NdegéOcello reflected very early in her career, "I'm not gay enough? I'm not black enough? I don't care."[27]

The critical "bi" or doubleness we see in *Plantation Lullabies* can be traced along its dual narratives which play out in the soundtrack, on one hand, and in the visual track, on the other. The album is literally bisexual, sometimes articulating a heterosexual set of relations and other times implying a same-sex aesthetic. These multiple sexualities do not undermine one another, but rather nuance how we might understand them individually. What I find interesting about NdegéOcello's bisexual politics are the black nationalist dimensions it takes in her first album, especially in light of the work she did after *Plantation Lullabies*.[28] Struggling to voice desire for identities often narrativized as mutually exclusive, NdegéOcello's album lapses into a black love rhetoric that habitually invokes the language of black nationalism. Which leads me to wonder: Is there a language of black love that isn't nationalist or at least won't sound nationalist when made to ride a beat? Even when NdegéOcello articulates her sexuality and her sexual aesthetic, she does so in the lingua franca of hip-hop: "gay life, the whole gay lifestyle . . . is patterned off a white gay male aesthetic. No that ain't my vibe . . . I love my brothers. I love my sisters. I am sexually functional with both."[29] The mark of how invested our understanding of what NdegéOcello says here, and how inflected it is by black nationalist slang, can be seen through her use of the terms "brothers" and "sisters." Of course she isn't talking about people she is related to; but she is using the "common sense" language of black nationalism to talk about men and women. Once again, as I have shown repeatedly in this study, a black queer politics is articulated in nationalist terms. The contemporary language of blackness is always already nationalist in its articulation.

The emphasis on nationalism in her first album, however, can also be read as a discomfort with articulating same-sex desire by masking it in ambiguity. In her essay "What Is Not Said: A Study in Textual Inversion," Diana Collecott discusses "lesbian silence" in texts, pointing out that the emphasis on "gayness" as male "leaves the lesbian conscious of herself as an absence from discourse, and the lesbian writer, teacher or theorist in an historical position that does not synchronize with the relative recognition and the relative freedom of gay men to write, teach and theorize."[30] I think we could apply Collecott's statement about lesbian identity to bisexual identity as well, especially if we consider that NdegéOcello vocalizes a heterosexual narrative, but shades her same-sex lyrics in ambiguity. In the case of NdegéOcello, we can read her "absence from discourse" as a bisexual as a result of the privileging of a black male nationalist politics. And, though her same-sex politics and eroticism seem to be submerged in the album's explicitly nationalist agenda, other aspects of the album as a material object suggest a counter-discursive thread that revises what on the surface appears to be an uncritical black nationalist approach. In her essay "Toward a Black Feminist Criticism," Barbara Smith notes that "if in a woman writer's work a sentence refuses to do what it is supposed to do, if there are strong images of women and if there is a refusal to be linear, the result is innately lesbian literature."[31] This notion might also be applied to NdegéOcello's work, which though not "literature," functions as a woman's cultural text which we might say does not do "what it is supposed to do" and refuses linearity and presents a strong image of women.

It is possible, then, to read the persistence of a problematic nationalism in *Plantation Lullabies* not as its devotion to nationalist discourses, but instead as a highlighting of its anxiety about race, gender, and sexuality and about how to articulate a "revolutionary" racial and sexual politics. This complicated play on nationalism is clear in the images, which function as a counternarrative to the ostensible heterosexism of some of the tracks on the album. These politics are illustrated in an image of an androgynous caricatured black face with white circles for eyes and lips invoking minstrelsy, on a yellow background with a red circle with a line through it, and the album's serial number is reproduced eight times in the top left hand corner (figure 1.1). This image suggests the album's break with negative stereotypes of black performance, telling us that on this album we will not find "typical" depictions of blackness and warning us that these are forbidden. The red prohibitive circle is a universal symbol and a command, clearly enacting the album's political boundaries. The repetitive reproduction of the serial number suggests the mechanism of capitalism at play in the performance of stereotypes of blackness as entertainment. It is an image that "jives" with the nationalist politics of the lyrics in songs like "Soul on Ice," but ultimately one that is less important than the other images, which speak to each other not only about race, but also about gender and sexuality.

The nationalism (and hence the spoken heterosexuality and unarticulated same-sex desire) of the album, however, is compromised by its visual subtext. In the clearest black-and-white photograph of her in the CD booklet, NdegéOcello wears a man's suit, with suspenders showing. Beneath this picture (figure 1.2) in minuscule print is the definition of her last name, explaining that NdegéOcello is a Swahili word meaning "free like a bird." In this picture, NdegéOcello performs the butch aesthetic, and this, paired with the definition of her name, suggests that she is "free" to love whomever she chooses and to look however she chooses. This is particularly significant in the context of her claim that her music is hip-hop because one reviewer contests this by saying, "So, anyway, I don't do non–Hip Hop reviews, [but] look man, *she* claims she's Hip Hop,"[32] indicating that it never occurred to him that NdegéOcello music was actually hip-hop. In this way, the reviewer puts on NdegéOcello the burden of "proof" that she is hip-hop, rather than legitimizing her claim to hip-hop through his review. In this way, he lets us know that even though he is reviewing her, her music isn't *really* hip-hop. What I'm getting at here is that by throwing her album into question through concerns related to genre, what he is actually doing is suggesting that there is no such thing as queer hip-hop. This heavily policed category of hip-hop is one that NdegéOcello's images expose as particularly exclusionary in the assumption that hip-hop is synonymous with masculinity.

Figure 1.1

Another black-and-white picture of her in the suit (figure 1.3), with half of her face cut off, has Greg Tate's famous poem about "alternative hip-hop" superimposed on top of it. While the other photograph shows a disheveled and playful-looking NdegéOcello, this one shows the suit fully buttoned and arranged, with no smile on her lips (which, along with the nose, are the only parts of her face we see) which serves to desexualize her body—she could be either male or female given the visual information this photograph provides us about her body. Tate says, "There is no such thing as alternative hip-hop," which her album undercuts, since her form of hip-hop is nothing like that of many of the more visibly identifiable male figures in the art form. At stake in her claim to hip-hop is the fact that she is a woman in an artistic field that is seen as being primarily male, and which is usually thought to articulate black male dissatisfaction and rage.[33] Tate defines hip-hop as

Figure 1.2

"James Brown's pelvis digitally grinded into technomorphine." And earlier he tells us that a "grim little sister" says, "There is no alternative hip-hop." Hence Tate's claim that "the only known alternative to hip-hop is dead silence." By replicating Tate's definition of hip-hop as radical in the visual liner notes here, NdegéOcello extends the radical implication of Tate's words to include the possibility of the articulation of a queer identity. If, as Tate maintains, "Hiphop is the inverse of capitalism / Hiphop is the reverse of colonialism," how does hip-hop (or can hip-hop) reverse or invert sexual and gender identity? This hip-hop discourse, superimposed on NdegéOcello in a suit, marks her trespass of forms of male expression, power, and privilege. As much as her soundtrack articulates a black nationalist and therefore inherently male discourse, the images in the CD booklet undermine the heterosexism of the very nationalist discourse some of her songs seem to endorse.

There's no such thing as alternative hiphop because
the only known alternative to hiphop
is dead silence.

The grim little sister in the black raincoat stepped up to the mic and said,
"I WANT Y'ALL TO REPEAT AFTER ME! THERE'S NO SUCH THING
AS ALTERNATIVE HIPHOP. THERE'S NO SUCH THING
AS ALTERNATIVE HIPHOP!"

Hiphop is the inverse of capitalism
Hiphop is the reverse of colonialism

Hiphop is the world the slaveholder made,
sent into niggafide future shock.

Hiphop is the black aesthetic by-product of the American dream machine,
our culture of consumption, commodification and subliminal seduction...
where George Clinton was out to warn us about Madison Ave.
urge overkill, the pimping of the pleasure principle...

Hiphop is the first Black musical movement in history that black people
pimped before the white boys got to it.

Hiphop converted raw soul into a fetishized commodity.

Hiphop has no morals, no conscience and no ecological concern
for the scavenged earth or the scavenged American minds
wrecked in its pursuit of new markets.

Unlike Sigourney Weaver's nemesis Alien, hiphop is not the other man's
rape fantasy of the black sex machine gone berserk.

Hiphop is James Brown's pelvis digitally grinded into technomorphine.

Hiphop is DOPE-KNOW-LOGY, THE ONLY KNOWN ANTIDOTE
FOR PRIME TIME SENSORY DEPRIVATION.

©1993 GREG TATE

Figure 1.3

There is, however, some ambiguity encoded in the notion that there is no alternative hip-hop.

While the reading I just produced above is one way to understand Tate's statement, it could also be read as a way of *including* all forms of hip-hop and normalizing them, rather than as excluding non-masculinist forms of hip hop. By superimposing Tate's words on her body, NdegéOcello could be suggesting that she is not an alternative hip-hop, she *is* hip-hop—that indeed, there is no such thing as alternative hip-hop because it should always be understood as articulating the angst of those who occupy the margins. In this way, NdegéOcello could be answering critics such as Charles Isbell (quoted above) who say she isn't hip-hop by using one of hip-hop's most famous and respected scribes to legitimate her project as hip-hop, or in other words, as legitimately and authentically "black." The ambiguous play on the line "there is no such thing as alternative hip-hop" mimics the album's renegotiation of race politics and an outlawed homosexuality.

Significantly, the booklet also reproduces Tate's famous line about hip-hop on two separate images. The first part of the line, "alternative hip-hop," is reproduced in larger letters across an image of a naked NdegéOcello wearing a necklace of cotton plants (figure 1.4). This image reminds us of slavery—of the auction block where black people where paraded in the nude, and of the forced labor of cotton picking, and significantly of the exploitation women suffered under slavery. It exposes NdegéOcello's breasts, which invoke the iconography of degraded black female sexuality.[34] Her hands and face are painted and she is lit to look blue-toned. Her hands and face are upturned, in a pose suggestive of suffering and pain. This image of female exposure and suffering, bearing a symbolic albatross of black oppression (cotton), produces dynamic tension with the ease (playful) and confidence (serious) in the black-and-white pictures of NdegéOcello in men's attire. Femininity, through the symbolic signification of this series of images, is distressed and yearning while masculinity is powerful and contained. Despite NdegéOcello's replication of Tate's statement, this last image contradicts Tate's notion by suggesting that black women's hip-hop production *is* alternative, and is another way of knowing black experience from that of masculine hip-hop discourses. The superimposition of the words "alternative hip-hop" on this image invites us to make the connection that this suffering black and female body—that the articulation of its truths—is alternative hip-hop. Through the images, NdegéOcello ostensibly interrogates Tate's claims about hip-hop, challenging the construction of it as male ("Hip-hop is James Brown's pelvis"), and critiquing the way in which it ignores black women's suffering. By exposing her breast in this image, NdegéOcello reminds us at once of race and of sex, of gender and of sexuality. It is an image that undermines the soundtrack and deconstructs the image of her in a suit, showing the efficacy of donning male attire while at the same time subverting the notion of fixed gender performance and identification. The latter part of this quote, "is dead silence," is either three or four images away from the first part of it (depending on which way you count) and is simply text highlighted by a graphic of black and white dots (figure 1.5). In this way, the notion that there is no alternative hip-hop is undermined by the fact that there is no image to accompany it. The placement of it, and the lack of visual complexity of its graphics, demonstrates that the overall album ultimately disagrees with Tate's masculinist and exclusionary definition of hip-hop. If one reads from the front of the CD booklet to the back, Tate's statement becomes a question: "Is dead silence alternative hip-hop?" This ordering, and the images that accompany the question, suggest that to say so is to silence the voices of black women who do indeed participate in an "alternative hip-hop," especially an alternative queer hip-hop which is the unspoken and submerged suggestion of the previously discussed songs and of the images of NdegéOcello in men's attire.[35]

Despite the subversive nature of the images in the CD booklet, and the questions about gender, sexuality and hip-hop they implicitly raise, NdegéOcello's songs themselves articulate a black nationalist politics of heterosexual "black love" and a well-rehearsed nationalist critique of interracial relationships. The incongruity of the soundtrack and the liner images suggests an ambivalent desire for acceptance by the predominantly black and male hip-hop community and so articulates a race politics that demonstrates that despite her bisexuality, NdegéOcello is "down for the black man." The images are at odds with the desire for "authentic" blackness that in a nationalist context, as I demonstrated earlier, is synonymous with heterosexuality. *Plantation Lullabies* is a good example of the way in which a text can at once engage nationalism while undermining it. It demonstrates that authors interested in resisting narratives of racism, gender, and sexuality can at once reject nationalism and endorse it, ably illustrating that while black nationalism "resists both the state and its social and racialized domination," it also "reinscribes the state in particular places within its own narratives of resistance."[36] This contradiction and complication, in the context of NdegéOcello's album, is metaphorized in its title, which invokes the nightmare of the plantation while signifying a double meaning through the word "lullaby," imbuing the title with images of horror and comfort, forced labor and soothing sleep, pain and relief from pain. It is precisely this double invocation that is at once mimesis and departure that complicates allegiance, politics, and the articulation of a radical hermeneutics that is performed by the renegotiated nationalism evident in NdegéOcello's *Plantation Lullabies*. These questions and contradictions of nationalism, which are so central to

Figure 1.4

the ongoing discussion of the articulation of black identity, continue to require examination.

Before concluding, I would like to briefly mention another instance of what I call a "recuperative rhythm" and a "negotiated nationalism" in the hip-hop world. Since NdegéOcello's bold moves in *Plantation Lullabies,* there have been some radical developments in the world of queer hip-hop. The rap group Deep/Dickollective (D/DC), for example, comprises three black out gay men whose music articulates what they might call a "BourgieBohoPostPomoAfroHomo" aesthetic.[37] The ideology espoused by the group is at once queer and nationalist; there is a strong critique of racism, a powerful claiming of black identity and beauty, and also endless references to black gay literature, films, and subculture. D/DC was formed in 2000, after the three men met at a screening of Marlon Riggs's film *Tongues Untied.* Going by the MC

Figure 1.5

names of pointfivefag, 25percenter, and The Lightskindid Phil/oso-
pher, the group confronts homophobia, racism, sexism, and classism
in all of their music. The symbolism used by the group pays homage
to the icons of black gay American culture. Their first album featured
an image of James Baldwin on the CD, and their latest album, *On Some
Other*, features Audre Lorde and Essex Hemphill on the album cover.

The negotiated nationalism articulated by D/DC is one that argues
for blackness without leaving any part of the queer self behind. On
the song "Babylon," 25percenter begins his verse by saying "I lives in
Zion,"[38] which is common parlance among Rastafarians and references
the idea of redemption and freedom from the racist system of oppression. But 25percenter indicates that the Zion he imagines is one that is
also free of homophobia: "jah why dem no let me peoples live to live
. . . blacqueer than black/cuz early one morn in '72 me was born

like dat." The "blacqueer" here sounds like "blacker," and radically reclaims blackness as queer, linguistically teasing out the queer locution in the word "blacker." He goes on to critique nationalism itself, "bass akward logic spent interceptin nationalisms," then articulates a vision of utopia based on egalitarian tolerance:

> boychilren in skirts / tomboys wit scuffs from dirt / spirits hurt / I help to heal with zeal by bein self to self / bump what another wanna do wit him monkey
> her dugout, hip, booty or mouth / my deep dic swing from limb to limb like Tarzan but with nappy napps tho / and a blakk man / negritude this string of metaphors like Fanonian holy wars against colonialists / th ish! / activist rap cat propositionin queer rebs / to grow fros and dreds to intimidate white house gates like F.O.I. / my kin be lesbo, drag queens, hetero, and bi / reverse the direction of the boom bye-bye without resortin to tit for tat / stand strong lil ones, me gats guns /spits rounds of verbage against haters / Zion is Mariposa luv strong chek ya data / dem my twenty-five cents out til later

In 25percenter's world people can be who they are—boychildren in skirts / tomboys in scuffs—without fear of "interceptin nationalisms." His string of metaphors references a range of black popular culture signifiers—Frantz Fanon, Tarzan, Zion, afros and dreadlocks—all while insisting upon gender and sexual freedom for the black queer subject. But even as interrogative and critical of homophobia and a variety of other "isms" as D/DC is, some problematic nationalist ideology remains. Take, for example, the mention of the F.O.I. in the quote above. As reference to the Nation of Islam's security force, the Fruit of Islam, this seems a discordant image to me, given the Nation of Islam's homophobic objections to homosexuality. Could it be that D/DC imagines a nation where no one is outside, not even, say, members of the F.O.I.; where Nation of Islam members would band together with blacqueer-than-black folks and "intimidate white house gates"? Is this a moment of transcendence, like the one Reid-Pharr talks about in his essay, that something like the Million Man March can achieve despite itself?

Samuel Delany complicates the term "nation," and ostensibly nationalism, by noting:

> Nation is a metaphor. If we talk about black communities, we're suddenly speaking about something more vulnerable than we

> would if we were speaking about nation . . . a nation is something that can raise an army . . . a community is something that is legally refused the raising of an army. So I think that when we use the metaphor of nation in a national situation, it functions as a metaphor to suppress or turn the focus away from our vulnerability.[39]

Delany's comment illustrates that the term "nation" functions as a shield to deflect attention away from the oppressed community. Assumption of dominant terminology by oppressed communities, he seems to suggest, is a tool or a weapon against the forces that suppress and threaten these marginalized communities. The use of "nation," then, is a tactic more than a description; it is a defensive gesture in the face of an offending system, in the face of a literal and *armed* nationalism. Just as nationalism cannot be completely dismissed—not only because of continuing oppression but also because of what it has accomplished (as Fusco so astutely points out)—it is bound to be important for defining whatever "new" concept we use to define our struggle for liberation. The most, it seems from the texts I have examined here, that can be imagined at this moment is *another* kind of *country* or nation; this is at once specific and ambiguous. "Another" is mutable and suggests myriad possibilities for change and space for the articulation of panoptical identities; while the word "country" implies borders, inherently necessitating an inside and its negative opposite, an outside. *Plantation Lullabies* and D/DC suggest that it is likely that the future holds some of both.

# "NO TENDER MERCY"

## SAME-SEX DESIRE,
## INTERRACIALITY,
## AND THE BLACK NATION

*There is no tender mercy for men of color, for sons who love men.*

—Essex Hemphill, Tongues Untied

*Nationalism . . . assigned everyone his place in life, man and woman, normal and abnormal, native and foreigner; any confusion between these categories threatened chaos and loss of control.*

—George Mosse, *Nationalism and Sexuality*

*We hold these truths to be self-evident, that all men are created equal; that they are endowed by their Creator with certain unalienable rights; that among these are life, liberty and the pursuit of happiness.*

—"The Black Panther Platform: What We Want,
What We Believe"

In 1997, Eddie Murphy was videotaped by Los Angeles sheriff deputies at 4:45 AM picking up Atisone Seiuli, a "beautiful Hawaiian-looking woman," and a known transsexual prostitute with a warrant out for her arrest. He would later explain that he was just "helping" the prostitute, telling KNBC-TV of Los Angeles that "I love my wife and I'm not gay . . . I'm married with three children."[1] Murphy's rebuttal to these charges, that he is "married with three children," engages discourses of reproduction as the antithesis of gayness, speaking to nationalist notions of the role and function of sex and sexuality.

Because interracial same-sex eroticism is figured, I argue, in opposition to black nationalist discourse, this incident—which not only potentially demonstrated Murphy's preference for transsexuals, but perhaps also could be read as an illustration of his preference for non-black people—threatened to invalidate Murphy not only as a heterosexually potent man, but also as a black cultural icon because homosexuality is regarded as an invalidation of authentic "blackness."[2] This incident, and Murphy's answer to it, is symptomatic of the ongoing project of "straightening out" the black community and, importantly, the impossibility of doing so. Benedict Anderson has famously argued that nations are "imagined communities" and in this case Murphy imagines that his status as father invalidates any same-sex desire he may feel or act on, thereby solidifying him as a "family man" and a "proper" subject of the community-nation. The irony of this incident, in the context of this monograph, is that in Marlon Riggs's *Tongues Untied* Murphy is cited as participating in the kind of homophobia that is most pejorative, since he has tremendous power to affect popular thinking about issues like homosexuality. Murphy's disavowals of gayness rely on nationalist tropes of the family as the ultimate symbol of racial and sexual order to validate his claim to heterosexuality. Other critics also perceived this incident as an important moment in popular culture because, as E. Patrick Johnson notes in his monograph, *Appropriating Blackness: Performance and the Politics of Authenticity,* it exposes something about the "leakage of black heterosexuality and masculinity."[3] This incident illustrates that as a primary metaphor of nationalism, reproduction becomes the index of "acceptable" desire.

Nationalism is most threatened by the prospect of its own extinction. George Mosse, as suggested by the above epigraph, notes that this threat is controlled through the production of "respectable" categories of identification and desire. Deviating from these categories established by nationalist discourse is threatening to its stability and perpetuation. These dichotomies ensure the reproduction of the nation through "appropriate" sex, which is sex that does not engage interracial or same-sex eroticism. Miscegenation and homosexuality obviously worry this equation. My discussion of interracial and same-sex desire turns on an understanding of nationalism that recognizes the importance of reproduction as a stabilization of national identity. This is not a new argument; Siobhan Somerville argues quite eloquently in *Queering the Color Line,* for example, that racial intermixture was thought to "have dangerous social and biological consequences."[4] She goes on to link discourses about miscegenation to the construction of homosexuality. Sexual acts are "perverse" when they do not serve the purpose of reproducing a homogeneous (sexually and racially) nation. In this chapter, I do not seek to explore the relationship between the desire for racial purity in the context of Eurocentric nationalism, but rather to show that similar concerns shape and inform black nationalist discourse about homosexuality and about miscegenation.

Though black nationalism saw itself as contrary to the aims of Eurocentric nationalism, the relationship between the two cannot be so easily disavowed, as the epigraph from "The Black Panther Platform: What We Want, What We Believe" clearly demonstrates. Taken directly from the Declaration of Independence, this passage confirms that the goals of black nationalism are predicated on the American ideal of "rights" as "unalienable" and God-given. It is significant that this passage is not *quoted* in the platform, but included as if it were native to that document.[5] It establishes that the Black Panther Party relied on a founding mainstream American principle to articulate their discontent with that very system. It is ironic, of course, that they are demanding the very things the Declaration of Independence purports to give all American citizens but fails to do because of systemic and institutionalized racism. But they are also bound to articulate their claims for "life, liberty and the pursuit of happiness" because these are the parameters set by Thomas Jefferson in 1776, and because—despite their attempts to disavow it—they are Americans. Hence the desire for a different politics is hindered by the anachronism of the nationalist movement's premise that the ideals upon which the United States is founded entitle all *men* to certain rights. In other words, the platform does not engage the entire range of possibility of the Declaration, but rather mobilizes around the rights of *men* while continuing to exclude women.[6] This is a fitting metaphor for my argument that the politics of black nationalism do not markedly contrast with Eurocentric nationalism(s) because the project of resistance is one that is always already bound to the oppressive system which creates the need for a politics of antithesis. As one writer so eloquently put it, "To oppose something is to maintain it."[7]

Black nationalism not only sees itself as contending for "liberty," but also for that other fundamental constitutional right, life. Black nationalism's worst-case scenario is that of extinction; and this fear is commonly asserted at the site of black masculinity. And so like Eurocentric nationalist discourse, black nationalism mobilizes around the question of reproduction and the threat of extinction (or death). The historical precedents for the threat to the perpetuation of the black race are the middle passage and slavery. By invoking pathos around the suffering black (mostly male) body as a kind of psychic and in many cases physical death, black nationalism gives emotional and historical support to its claims about the threat of white supremacy, ignoring the fact, however, that American slavery *depended* upon the reproduction of black people as workers—not on their elimination.[8] Despite this oversight, the danger black people faced (and still do) was not imagined—it was, and is, real—but the response to this danger was enmeshed, like the notion of rights, with the epistemologies of Eurocentric nationalism. The solution to the threat of extinction, then, is to exist and continue to exist. The call for the reproduction of the nation through heterosexual and monoracial sex is one that is fundamental to black nationalist politics. Like Eurocentric nationalist discourses, black nationalism perceives threat through the trope of reproduction. Therefore, sexual acts that make impossible the birth of "black" children are denounced by black nationalism; like miscegenation, homosexuality is undesirable because, as both white and black homophobic thinking argues, it "endangers the normal development of our young toward their own duty to reproduce,"[9] arguing that same-sex desire is "selfish, unnatural, anathema to the building of a strong black nation."[10] Because it was thought to have no reproductive possibility, same-sex desire was seen as counter-productive to the aims of the nation. And since black nationalism saw white supremacy as a threat to the race, it metaphorized gayness as whiteness through the trope of endangered reproduction, arguing that "to endorse lesbianism was to endorse the death of our race,"[11] as Audre Lorde notes.

Importantly, the link between Eurocentric and black nationalisms can be further exposed through an examination of the patriarchal nature of both discourses. Sharon P. Holland has noted that in hip-hop the black male functions as the authentic site of suffering. The same is true of black nationalism, to which hip-hop is indebted in important aspects. Black nationalism is invested in the production of a patriarchal hegemony, where the black male body is the legitimate space of suffering[12] and where the ultimate reproductive aim of the nation is to reproduce not only blackness, but maleness. Black feminists have critiqued its repressive gender politics while not always recognizing that the sexual and racial politics of black nationalism are as deeply flawed as those of Eurocentric nationalism.[13] Perhaps black nationalism seduces because it offers the promise of homogeneity, even though this is a false solution to the iniquitous burdens of racism. So while black nationalism originally conceived of itself as opposing the agenda of Eurocentric nationalism, it actually reproduced it in a new context.

James Baldwin's *Another Country* reveals the fact that these discourses are so interdependent that our racial and sexual selves can never be homogeneous or circumscribed. There can be no "white" or "black" nation because the relationship of opposition between the two is what makes the idea of a racially pure (and reproductive) nation even possible. To write about same-sex interraciality is not only to contemplate but to perform these anxieties around reproduction of the nation. I will show that in these texts nationalism is critiqued *and* upheld through considerations of racial and sexual boundaries. I begin my discussion of these issues with Eldridge Cleaver's *Soul on Ice* because it articulates a nationalist critique of interraciality and homosexuality while, like Eddie Murphy, "not quite succeeding at asserting itself and the black community as straight,"[14] as Robert Reid-Pharr has noted in another context.

## "Have You Ever Wished You Were Queer?"[15]

> The object of one's hatred is never, alas, conveniently outside but seated in one's lap, stirring in one's bowels and dictating the beat of one's heart.
>
> —James Baldwin, "Here Be Dragons"

Eldridge Cleaver's 1968 essay "Notes on a Native Son" is now infamous for its attack on James Baldwin. Cleaver enunciates the interface of anxieties about interracial same-sex desire, and projects them onto Baldwin, when he states:

> The case of James Baldwin aside, it seems that many Negro homosexuals, acquiescing in this racial death-wish, are outraged and frustrated because in their sickness they are unable to have a baby

by a white man. The cross they bear is that, already bending over and touching their toes for the white man, the fruit of their miscegenation is not the little half-white offspring of their dreams but an increase in the unwinding of their nerves—though they redouble their efforts and intake of the white man's sperm.[16]

Cleaver must assert his masculinity in terms explicitly heterosexual. His discomfort is not only with homosexual desire, but also with submission to the white man. Notice his need to illustrate the black man "bending over and touching [his] toes" and the reference to the white man's orgasm. The "cross they bear" for Cleaver is not only their racial "death-wish" but the fact that they are "already bending over," emphasizing that Cleaver sees their thwarted desire for miscegenated offspring as an additional burden, as a bowing to white power and a continuation of the subjugation black men have historically suffered at the hands of whites. The black man is shamed because he is willing to submit to a white man. For Cleaver, this bending compromises one's negotiation of racism and one's masculinity. Cleaver's power dynamic is strongly tied to the issue of who is *the man.* That question of masculinity is resolutely implicated in Cleaver's racial discourse. He can only imagine black/white interraciality through a power paradigm in which black men are feminized:

> The black homosexual, when his twist is a racial nexus, is an extreme embodiment of contradiction. This white man has deprived him of his masculinity, castrated him in the center of his burning skull, and when he submits to this change and takes the white man as his lover as well as Big Daddy, he focuses on "whiteness" all the love in his pent up soul and turns the razor edge of hatred against "blackness"—upon himself, what he is, and those who look like him, [and who] remind him of himself.[17]

For Cleaver, to be both homosexual and black is to express a hatred for blackness through the death-wish. In this construction, to be black is to be feminized and to be gay is to be castrated. Homosexuality, then, is the ultimate threat to being *the man,* since it presumably takes away that which makes you one: the impregnating phallus. And interracial homosexuality ensures that *the man* will be white, which is precisely what Cleaver is fighting against; he claims for himself (or for black men) the position as *top* man. Taken together, these statements go directly to the metaphorical heart of the matter, namely that the (in)ability to reproduce is not only a concern in Cleaver's racial and sexual cosmology, but also, *he thinks,* a concern of the black gay man. In other words, while Cleaver critiques interracial same-sex desire as a death-wish, he is unable to maintain the idea that black gay men wish for the death of the race, since in the end he can't help figuring them as desiring reproduction, as wanting the "half-white fruit of miscegenation." His attempt to decry homosexuality, then, is one that is fraught with contradiction since he cannot render black gay men as innocent of the imperative (not unlike his own) to reproduce. This suggests that Cleaver does not see the gay black man as the ultimate "other" from himself or even as entirely free from the underlying goal of nationalism, which is to reproduce. His homophobia, then, can be read as a disavowal of his desire for Baldwin rather than a simple repudiation of him as a gay man. Others have also pointed out that Cleaver's diatribe against Baldwin masks (and thinly so) his desire for Baldwin. As E. Patrick Johnson so eloquently puts it, "Cleaver's rhetorical performance in 'Notes of a Native Son' . . . is a decoy for what lies elsewhere—deferred (unconsciously?) until sealed, made manifest, with a kiss. Indeed, in *Soul on Ice* Cleaver speaks the love that dare not speak its name in the very act of not speaking."[18]

Though Cleaver attempts to limit his characterization of same-sex desire as a death-wish, his own relationship to notions of reproduction is complicated by his desire to "sit on a pillow beneath the womb of Baldwin's typewriter and catch each newborn page as it entered this world of ours."[19] Cleaver's earlier reference to the black gay man's desire to have the white man's child is mimicked here when he demonstrates his desire to participate in Baldwin's (re)productivity. He is not convinced by his own argument that homosexuality is a death-wish since he is willing to be the midwife who serves as witness to Baldwin's (re) productive legacy. Cleaver's rejection of Baldwin is not a repudiation based merely in his identification of Baldwin as gay. His initial description of Baldwin shows all the earmarks of idolatry: "After reading a couple of James Baldwin's books, I began experiencing that continuous delight one feels upon discovering a fascinating, brilliant talent on the scene, a talent capable of *penetrating* so profoundly into one's own little world that one knows oneself to have been unalterably changed and *liberated,* liberated from the frustrating grasp of whatever devils happen to possess one." (emphasis mine)[20] Baldwin is given the highest compliment, that of having the ability to *penetrate* Cleaver's own little world and "free" him. The use of the verb "liberate" shows that Cleaver regards Baldwin as capable of breaking his bonds of oppression. Baldwin speaks to him racially: "a black . . . responds with an additional dimension of his being to the articulated experience of another black."[21] He goes on to say that he "lusted for anything that Baldwin had written" and "was delighted with Baldwin, with those great big eyes of his, which one thought to be fixedly focused on the macrocosm, could also *pierce* the microcosm"[22] (emphasis mine). Again Cleaver endows Baldwin with the ability to pierce, to penetrate, to cleave: his insistence on these verbs of power and their association with masculine sexuality indicate that Cleaver is, at best, ambivalent about Baldwin's sexuality. And his use of the word "lust" demonstrates the extent to which he desired to be pierced by Baldwin's wit and insight. That Cleaver is not afraid to use sexual language in his description of Baldwin, especially given that he spends the remainder of the article demonstrating his homophobia, contradicts the trajectory of that homophobia. His clear *love* of Baldwin is negated by the fact that Baldwin has rejected the *ideal* of black masculinity, an ideal with which Cleaver is strongly identified. His first verbal assault on Baldwin reflects the complicated nature of Cleaver's criticism of Baldwin, a criticism which is anchored in what Cleaver sees as Baldwin's racial and sexual self-hatred. He initially attacks Baldwin not in terms of his sexuality, but in racial terms, stating that Baldwin has a "grueling, agonizing, total hatred of the blacks, particularly of himself, and the most shameful, fanatical, sycophantic love of whites."[23] He brings up Baldwin's sexuality almost as an aside, bracketed in commas as a subordinate clause, in the context of the racial death-wish: "The case of James Baldwin aside for a moment, it seems that many Negro homosexuals [acquiesce] in this racial-death wish."[24] Baldwin becomes the template against which Cleaver defines all black gay men. As the essay progresses, however, his interest in Baldwin's sexuality, as the primary index of his racial self-hatred, grows. Cleaver's argument about black gay men is that their sexual "sickness" is paralleled and informed by their racial "sickness."

This is complicated by the fact that Cleaver conceptualizes same-sex desire as a contest of masculinity, a construction that will be reflected in Vivaldo and Rufus's relationship, which I discuss later in this chapter.

When Cleaver discusses Baldwin's critique of Richard Wright, he condemns Baldwin for being unable to "confront the stud" in Wright, noting that Baldwin "was not about to bow to a *black* man."[25] As homophobic as Cleaver's attack on Baldwin is, his primary rejection of Baldwin seems related to Baldwin's representation of erotic love between black and white men. Baldwin's homosexuality is attacked primarily because it is, as identified by Cleaver, an *interracial* homosexuality. In other words, Cleaver's peculiar argument seems to suggest that Baldwin's presumed rejection of black masculinity as sexually desirable is what is most objectionable. Despite his repudiation of homosexuality in the end—"Homosexuality is a sickness"[26]—Cleaver's essay not only represents a castigation of homosexuality, but stages its rejection in the context of *interracial* homosexuality, because he conceptualizes it as a rejection of the worth and value of black masculinity. He sees Baldwin as staging "an underground guerrilla war, waged on paper, against black masculinity"[27] and is driven into a vexed, and interracial, identification with a white man, Norman Mailer—which is exactly the kind of identification he accuses Baldwin of. Discursively, then, Cleaver has not created a politics of sexual and racial opposition to what he perceives as Baldwin's politics. Cleaver's repudiation of Baldwin thinly veils his deep identification with Baldwin and his characters.

The tension in Cleaver's essay around Baldwin's sexuality (and homosexuality in general) is related, I argue, to the homosocial bonds which characterize black nationalism. In essence, Cleaver cannot completely reject Baldwin's love of men since it is Cleaver's presumably nonerotic love of black men which drives his black nationalist agenda. It is, after all, black masculinity which he feels Baldwin is threatening, i.e., other black men he presumably loves (because they are black). Metaphorically, Cleaver feels that Baldwin has rejected *him,* if not erotically then nationalistically, and that Baldwin's crime is his love of whiteness as much as it is his love of men. It is love between men that cements the bonds of nationalism, as Eve Kosofsky Sedgwick has famously argued in *Between Men: English Literature and Male Homosocial Desire.*[28] She notes that women are exchanged as property to seal the bonds of men with men. Therefore, Cleaver's repudiation of Baldwin's homosexuality is discursively at odds with his black nationalism since nation building is about man building, and about homosocial space. Baldwin's stance against black nationalism, however, and Negritude is problematic for

Cleaver, as evidenced in his essay by Baldwin's unsympathetic attitude to the Conference of Black Writers and Artists. In Cleaver's cosmology, heterosexuality is important for the reproduction of the nation, and women are most important in their "prone" position. In other words, nationalism values little about women except their reproductive role in "building a strong black nation." It is not difficult to conclude that black nationalism, intellectually and politically, is primarily an affair between men. While Baldwin maintains an "anti-nationalist" standpoint, Cleaver maintains his homophobia. This relationship between Baldwin's homosexuality (and his depiction of it in his novels) and Cleaver's black nationalist politics suggests that each ideology is the antithesis of the other, an idea that is radically challenged and revamped in Marlon Riggs's *Tongues Untied,* a film that demonstrates, among other things, that homosexuality is not the equivalent of a racial death-wish and that there is and can be nationalist black gay discourse.

Cleaver sees the death of Rufus Scott in *Another Country* as a consummate example of Baldwin's death-wish. He argues that Baldwin "slandered" Rufus Scott, and Cleaver sees Rufus as a "weak, craven-hearted ghost."[29] Baldwin's crime is that he renders the only black man in *Another Country* a failure of the idealized vision of black masculinity imagined by Cleaver. It is through Rufus that we can examine the divide that separates the Cleaver of "Notes on a Native Son" and the Baldwin of *Another Country.* Cleaver's obsession with the character of Rufus Scott, who dies at the beginning of the novel, mimics the behavior of the characters in the novel, whose subsequent narratives are framed and informed by Rufus's life and death. The tendency to focus so exclusively on Rufus illustrates the power of the black male figure as the referent for masculinity, sexuality, and raciality. *Another Country* is a novel that implicitly confronts and critiques nationalist discourses. Thought about in the context of black nationalism, which is a discourse associated with and often espoused by men, *Another Country* is a meditation on the issues of nationalism drawing on the tropes of racial and sexual desire.

Cleaver's notion of a death-wish is one that resonates with *Another Country* because Rufus literalizes the death-wish by committing suicide. Laura Quinn writes in her essay "'What's Going On Here?': Baldwin's *Another Country*" that after only eighty-eight pages "*Another Country* . . . kills off its black male protagonist" and later describes Rufus's death as a "tragic suicide/sacrifice."[30] Figuring Rufus's death as "murder," enacted upon him by the text/author or by the effects of racism, is perhaps the most common way of thinking through Rufus's early textual demise. Even the characters in the novel (specifically Vivaldo) speculate that Rufus's death was caused by their and society's shortcomings. Terry Rowden argues that in *Another Country* "Baldwin's homosexual 'utopianism' is secured through the *scapegoating* of the black man" (emphasis mine).[31] While writers and critics like Samuel Delany would certainly object to the characterization of Baldwin's work that treats homosexuality as the creation of a gay "utopianism,"[32] this quote demonstrates that a significant amount of discussion about *Another Country*, and specifically about Rufus, is characterized by the notion that his death represents his status as victim. Sharon P. Holland notes in her essay "Bill T. Jones, Tupac Shakur and the (Queer) Art of Death" that the loss of the black masculine subject (her term is "fatherlack") represents the "authentic site of mourning for African Americans."[33] The critical attention Rufus's death receives invites us to realize the spectral power black masculinity has not only over the characters in the text, but also over the readers. A critique of this preoccupation is voiced by Richard in the novel when he says, "I couldn't help feeling, anyway, that one of the reasons all of you made such a kind of—fuss—over him was partly just because he was colored. Which is a hell of a reason to love anybody."[34] The novel invites our centripetal preoccupation with Rufus, his life and, importantly, his death by mapping all the sexual desire that follows through his character. At the same time, however, its ending—as I later show—offers a critique of the textual tendency to center Rufus and his experiences. Instead of considering why Rufus commits suicide, I seek here to show that *Another Country's* ending works against the notion of black masculinity as the consolidating index of difference. Rufus's death suggests that there is no black utopia, no place where he can escape the iniquities of racism. More importantly, *Another Country* implies that we have not yet found a model for thinking outside the box which frames our discussions of interraciality and same-sex eroticism. The title of the novel indicates the wish for "another country," another nation, in which our racial and sexual selves are imagined and defined differently, or perhaps where they are not defined at all. It is at once a question—another country?—illustrating the futility of national crossings; and it is a wistful fantasy: *another country,* a mythic, imaginary, and unattainable place where relationships are not fractured by difference but are productively bound together by it.

The critique of nationalism in *Another Country* is frequently missed in criticism about the novel, and as I noted above, there is a tendency to focus on the character of Rufus and his death. I do not mean to suggest, however, that this aspect of the novel is unworthy of attention. Indeed, if we follow Kathryn Bond Stockton's formulation in *Beautiful Bottom, Beautiful Shame* (2006), it seems inevitable that the consequence of Rufus's interracial same-sex desire would be death. For, following the framing language established by Cleaver, Stockton points out that in the case of interracial same-sex encounters "what could be bred was not a baby, but a corpse."[35] Rufus's death is important to explore because the death-wish is the index of sickness in Cleaver's cosmology, especially in relation to black masculinity, and it touches the nerves of the death of black innocence and love, demonstrating that for the black male subject interraciality is always the harbinger of death. Baldwin demonstrates the persuasive power of black masculinity by having his anti-hero govern the narrative from the grave. In this way the novel signifies on the obsession with black masculinity as the manifestation of the black nation.

Such signification characterizes the connubiality between Vivaldo and Rufus, and, I argue, the contest of masculinity that thwarts desire between them. This is most explicit right after Rufus and Leona get together. Vivaldo comes over the night after Rufus and Leona have had sex for the first time, and Rufus immediately finds himself thinking about what Vivaldo is thinking about him, *sexually:*

> He stole a look at Vivaldo, sipping his beer and watching Leona with an impenetrable smile . . . Perhaps Vivaldo was contemptuous of her because she was so plain—perhaps Vivaldo was contemptuous of him. Or perhaps he was flirting with her because she seemed so simple and available: the proof of her availability being her presence in Rufus' house.[36]

The parallel construction in the sentence, "contemptuous of him" and "contemptuous of her," marks Rufus's inability to differentiate between Vivaldo's probable desire for Leona and/or himself. Rufus is worrying about the boundaries of Vivaldo's desire. He is questioning his sexual value as a black man to a white man, whose sexuality is thought to have the most value. He wonders, in other words, if Vivaldo wants *him* or thinks *he* is "easy" because he is black. Rufus's fear that Vivaldo's desire for Leona is mediated by a racist assumption that she is available (and loose) because she is with a black man is his indirect way of wondering if Vivaldo considers *him,* a black man, a worthy sexual partner. The questions running through Rufus's mind about Vivaldo and sex may be less about sexual desire and more about wondering how close Vivaldo is willing to get to a black *man*. Would race, or masculinity, in the most exposed and naked space (the bedroom), separate them still? Gail Bederman's analysis of race and gender in *Manliness and Civilization* (1995) suggests that these aspects of gender and race "have worked in tandem . . . to complicate and exacerbate the cultural forces leading to racism."[37] As such, Rufus's appraisal of Vivaldo's reaction to Leona neatly maps the conjunction of gender and race in the production of Vivaldo's (perceived) racist reaction. Embodied in this question posed indirectly by Rufus is a contradiction, because race has never kept people from having sex. In this context, Leona and Rufus are sufficient evidence of that, as are Vivaldo and Ida. In fact, quite often the bedroom is where race is staged, performed, and indulged.[38] It is their competing masculinity that keeps Rufus and Vivaldo apart, matrixed as it is through race, and through homosexuality, even though both Rufus and Vivaldo sleep with Eric, but never with each other.

Rufus and Vivaldo are connected by sex, by the triangulated relations of their sex lives. After Rufus dies, Vivaldo remembers, "They had slept together, got drunk together, balled chicks together, cursed each other out, and loaned each other money."[39] The attraction between them is always deflected onto "chicks" they "balled together." Later Vivaldo realizes that these sexual trysts, between men involving the same women, have "very little to do with [the women]."[40] Vivaldo is ready to recognize that this is about an exchange, a tentative intercourse, among men. He then thinks to himself: "but neither could it be said that they had been trying to attract each other—they would never, certainly, have dreamed of doing it that way."[41] He is not ready, however, to acknowledge the ways in which sexual attraction might motivate such liaisons—and instead his mind returns to a consideration of masculinity. His use of "certainly" implies a disavowal of how men may try, through their sexual relations with women, to attract one another. Vivaldo would rather conceptualize these trysts as events meant to "set their minds at ease; at ease as to which of them was the better man,"[42] and *not* as examples of sexual attraction between himself and other men.

It is their loyalty to a fantasy of masculinity that bars the free flow of desire between them. Implicit in these questions of sex and masculinity is the idea of submission. As with Eldridge Cleaver, questions of submission are at stake between Rufus and Vivaldo. In other words, who will have the power—who will be *the man*—is the question standing between them. Vivaldo realizes this explicitly when he thinks, "well, perhaps they had been afraid that if they looked too closely into one another each would have found—he looked out of the window, feeling damp and frightened. Each would have found the abyss. Somewhere in his heart the black boy hated the white boy because he was white. Somewhere in his heart Vivaldo hated and feared Rufus because he was black."[43] It is a battle of patriarchies—it is two nationalisms fighting for primacy.

Despite all the ways in which Rufus is *not* a nationalist, black nationalism is embodied most forcibly in his character. As far as Cleaver is concerned, Rufus loses the contest because he participates in the "white man's pastime"[44] of committing suicide. From the perspective of black nationalist politics, Rufus's suicide is simply another way he fails as a black man. Despite Cleaver's delineation of Rufus's racial deficiencies, there is a striking parallel between Rufus and Cleaver in the sense that their erotic love for white women is contradicted and yet indelibly tied to their intense hatred of white authority, represented by white men. In the first chapter of *Soul on Ice,* Cleaver writes:

> At the moment I walked out of the prison gate, my feelings toward white women in general could be summed up in the following lines:
>
> > I love you
> > Because you're white,
> > Not because you're charming
> > Or bright.
> > Your whiteness
> > Is a silky thread
> > Snaking through my thoughts

In red-hot patterns
Of lust and desire.
I hate you
Because you're white.
Your white meat
Is nightmare food.
White is
The skin of Evil.
You're my Moby Dick,
White Witch,
Symbol of the rope and hanging tree
Of the burning cross.
Loving you thus
And hating you so,
My heart is torn in two.
Crucified.[45]

Rufus's feelings for Leona are not far from this love/hate dilemma expressed by Cleaver. Cleaver equates his love for a white woman with inevitable death through a reference to lynching. His mention of "the rope" and the "hanging tree" are bold allusions to one of the injustices black men suffered under slavery and Jim Crow. The love he expresses for her is due only to his self-hatred. His "love" for her is negated by the history of, and his experience with, American racism. This love/hate dichotomy characterizes Leona and Rufus's relationship as well. In the last conversation Vivaldo and Rufus have before Rufus's death, Rufus expresses intense hatred for white people:

> How I hate them—all those white sons of bitches out there. They're trying to kill me, you think I don't know? They got the world on a string, man, the miserable white cock suckers, and they tying that string around my neck, they killing *me*.[46]

Like Cleaver, the rope (or string) which characterizes whiteness is associated with death for Rufus. Both use the metaphor of lynching to capture the intensity of their feelings about racism. Vivaldo tells Rufus, after this monologue, that "not everybody's like that" and that "Leona loves you."[47] To which Rufus responds, "'She loves the colored folks so *much* . . . sometimes I just can't stand it. You know all that chick knows about me? The *only* thing she knows?' He put his hand on his sex, brutally, as though he would tear it out, and seemed pleased to see Vivaldo wince."[48] The link here between lynching and the violence enacted by Rufus to his penis is a painful reminder of the history of racial and sexual oppression represented by lynching. Lynching is a sexual and racial crime, perpetuated on black (usually male) bodies and frequently including mutilation. It is a dangerous conflation of desire and national anxiety, sparked by the threat of a competing masculinity.

What recent discourse about lynching has taught us is that the act itself speaks not to black threat, but to growing nationalist anxieties about whiteness and the perpetuation of it. Robyn Wiegman has argued that "not only does lynching enact a grotesquely symbolic—if not literal—sexual encounter between the white mob and its victim, but the increasing utilization of castration as a preferred form of mutilation for African American men demonstrates lynching's connection to the sociosymbolic realm of sexual difference."[49] In this way, Rufus forcefully reminds Vivaldo of precisely what it is that separates him from Leona and Vivaldo: racism, and specifically, the history of violence it embodies and the continued threat of it. Though Rufus commits suicide, the novel invites us to read his corpus (both what he says about his breath being cut off by the "string" of racism and his actual body) against the historical echo of Emmett Till. Baldwin's pain over Till's death is well-known in regard to his award-winning play *Blues for Mister Charlie* (1964). Ida's description of her brother's body after it is pulled from the river, however, suggests that the image of Till's battered body was not far from Baldwin's mind:

> When we saw Rufus's body, I can't tell you. My father stared at it, he stared at it, and stared at it. It didn't look like Rufus, it was—terrible—from the water, and he must have *struck* something going down, or in the water, because he was so broken and lumpy—and ugly. *My* brother.[50]

This description sounds much like the photographs of Till that were published to much controversy in *Jet* magazine. Rufus becomes an "it" in Ida's telling of the story; Rufus becomes the general black male corpse, battered and swollen and maimed by racism. Understanding Rufus's death as a metaphorical lynching and as connected to the death of Emmett Till, who was also killed because of the threat of the interracial, brings Ida's own name into focus—since Ida B. Wells was a well-known figure in the fight against lynching.[51] As Jacqueline Goldsby argues in her monograph *A Spectacular Secret: Lynching in American Life and Literature* (2006), lynching's "far-reaching violence shaped the nation's cultural life."[52] And about Emmett Till in particular, Goldsby notes that his murder "haunts our national conscience" unlike any other.[53] Thus Rufus's death connects to the culture of black male death by the framing of his body in a river and maimed beyond recognition.

Rufus's invocation of lynching is also strikingly similar to Cleaver's in his poem from *Soul on Ice*. The parallel between Rufus's character and Cleaver's persona in *Soul on Ice* is significant because it signals similar conflicts, staged around questions of homosexuality, nationalism, and race. The discourse of black nationalism is submerged in characterization in *Another Country,* as is the question of same-sex desire in *Soul on Ice*.

Laura Quinn has pointed out that *Another Country* starts with a tortured heterosexual, interracial relationship (Rufus and Leona) and ends with a monoracial, homosexual one (Yves and Eric). There is nothing, however, she argues, to suggest that this relationship will "work" any better than the others in the novel.[54] It is significant, though, that Yves is arriving in New York, in America, from *another country*. He is optimistic despite his earlier reticence about his and Eric's relationship:

> He looked up. Eric leaned on the rail of the observation deck, grinning, wearing an open white shirt and khaki trousers. He looked very much at ease, at home, thinner than he had been, with his short hair spinning and flaming about his head. Yves looked up joyously, and waved, unable to say anything. *Eric.* And all his fear left him, he was certain, now, that everything would be all right.[55]

Yves is both arriving *from* and *to* another country; this suggests that his movement from one emotional state (reluctance and fear) to another (joy and certainty) represents a literal and emotional emigration from one country to another. It is significant that a novel called *Another Country* ends with a French citizen arriving in New York. His voyage across the Atlantic is met by Eric, who with his hair "spinning and flaming" about his head, mimics the Statue of Liberty, whose halo of spikes might be described as "spinning and flaming." The sight of

Eric inspires within Yves the same hope the Statue of Liberty is said to inspire in immigrants. But the novel has taught us to be skeptical, as skeptical as we are of the "American Dream," and we know that if Yves and Eric are lucky then they might achieve "a maximum of relief with a minimum of hostility."[56] This suggests that despite the seemingly homogeneous nature of the relationship, difference still must be negotiated. We are invited to see difference embodied beyond Rufus, or beyond the boundaries of interraciality. It is not an ending that disavows black masculinity, but instead one that de-centers it as the defining trope of racial and sexual difference. This ending sets up considerations that rearrange the black/white, male/female paradigms of difference. Even as *Another Country* encourages us to look not only to the character of Rufus for the whelps of race and sex, it complicates this trajectory in the novel by conjuring a cathartic response from its characters and readers for black life.

# (NOT) LOVING HER

## A LOCUS OF CONTRADICTIONS

*Blackness [is] that reclaiming of culture, that will to revolution; embracing the remarkable and violated past, the very tenuous present, and the unpromised future as an African in diaspora, an ex-slave, lesbian, poet.*
—Cheryl Clarke

*So, Afrekete is . . . and Afrekete ain't.*
—Catherine McKinley, Introduction, *Afrekete*

The introduction to *Afrekete: An Anthology of Black Lesbian Writing* (1995) highlights the importance of race in the lives of black lesbians. The editors, Catherine E. McKinley and L. Joyce DeLaney, define Afrekete as "a perfect creation of the Black lesbian feminist imagination."[1] The term alludes to a character in Audre Lorde's autobiographical novel, *Zami: A New Spelling of My Name* (1982). In *Zami*, Afrekete, a young black lesbian from the South who is new to the New York social scene, helps Lorde heal from the breakup with her white partner. Afrekete is important in *Zami* as a narrative device used by Lorde to claim a specifically black lesbian identity. The character Afrekete demonstrates that inherent and native lesbianism is also the domain of black women, hence rejecting the homophobic logic which renders same-sex desire "white" (a matter I discuss at great length in chapter 1). At stake in *Afrekete*'s title is a similar claiming of the black lesbian space. Underlying "Afrekete" in her multiple manifestations (in Lorde's novel as character, in the anthology as title) is the notion of black-on-black lesbian love and a need to naturalize black lesbian identity.

The particular rhetorical strategy used by the editors of *Afrekete,* evidenced by the second epigraph above, references Marlon Riggs's film *Black Is/Black Ain't* (1994), whose title, of course, is itself a quote from Ralph Ellison's *Invisible Man* (1952). It is no coincidence that Riggs uses Ellison's language to rethink blackness as a category since during the 1960s Ellison came under attack by black nationalists in much the same way writers like Baldwin were maligned for representing same-sex desire. As Henry Louis Gates Jr. points out in his essay "The Black Man's Burden," "James Baldwin and Ralph Ellison were victims of the Black Arts movement of the 1960's, the former for his sexuality, the latter for his insistence upon individualism."[2] It seems apt, then, that Riggs would invoke Ellisonian individualism to rebut the idea of a universalizing, essential blackness. Riggs's film complicates notions of black identity along class, color, and sexual lines. It rejects an essential blackness, offering the metaphor of gumbo—a diverse pot of deliciousness—to map the diversity of blackness.

In *Invisible Man,* the line "black is and black ain't" is spoken by a preacher in a marijuana-induced dream sequence experienced by the protagonist. The phrase accurately performs the theoretical position of blackness. As Jennifer DeVere Brody astutely notes in her essay "The Blackness of Blackness . . . Reading the Typography of *Invisible Man*":

> The embodied experience is played out against a series of always already inscribed notions of what blackness "is" and "ain't" and of our expectations of its overdetermined value. That blackness is invisible—is tied to the ocular—is the premise that Ellison's famous novel at once seeks to acknowledge and undo through its complicated rendering of scenes that stage and restage formative moments of blackness in American culture.[3]

Therefore, we might always understand allusions to *Invisible Man*'s "is/ain't" construction as signaling a "formative moment" in relation to identity. The rhetorical work done by "black is" plays on the idea of the "fact" of blackness, while "black ain't" indicates the constructed nature of race and the mutability of any designation related to it.[4] It speaks to the paradox of race confronted in Ellison's novel—that blackness is so hypervisual (it is all anyone sees who looks at the protagonist) that it renders one invisible (they cannot see him, he is invisible as an individual). The second half of the phrase does not undo the first by emptying blackness of all indicative power. Instead, the phrase functions to reify blackness as heterogeneous and diverse. So when the editors of *Afrekete* deploy the phrase, they perform a double racial claiming: first, by referencing Lorde's character Afrekete and then by using this well-known phrase that points to the only unifying principle of "blackness," which is its sundry mutability. In both the invocation of Afrekete and the reference to the "is/ain't" configuration, the explicit goal of the editors is to ground their lesbianism in blackness.

This anchoring of lesbianism in blackness arises out of the invisibility of the black lesbian, in black life as well as in mainstream lesbian circles. If it is true, as has been theorized by black feminist critics, that the black woman is erased in black nationalist discourse and in mainstream feminist discourse—that she suffers under the double bind of gender oppression and racism—then the black lesbian is even further away from the center, an unimaginable, unfathomable, unutterable entity. Evelyn Hammonds speaks to this invisibility when she writes:

> Black women's sexuality is often described in metaphors of speechlessness, space, or vision, as a "void" or empty space that is simultaneously ever visible (exposed) and invisible and where black women's bodies are always already colonized.[5]

Hammonds goes on to argue that this invisibility is compounded when the black woman is a lesbian, where the only paradigmatic lens for thinking about black lesbians is through white lesbian sexualities. She argues that this "tends to obfuscate rather than illuminate the subject position of black lesbians."[6] Hammonds is not alone in her identification of the black lesbian's discursive invisibility. Jewelle Gomez has written of this silence as a "shadow of repression" that has "concealed the Black Lesbian in literature in proportion to her invisibility in American society."[7] And Ann Allen Shockley, whose book *Loving Her* is the subject of this chapter, names this lack as well:

> Until recently, there has been almost nothing written by or about the Black Lesbian in American literature—a deficiency suggesting that the Black Lesbian was a nonentity in imagination as well as in reality. This unique Black woman, analogous to Ralph Ellison's "invisible man," was seen but not seen because of what the eyes did not wish to behold.[8]

Shockley's reference to *Invisible Man* ties into the paradox of identity which the editors of *Afrekete* and Marlon Riggs use to complicate and assert black same-sex desire. In the context of this issues, we can see why Ann Allen Shockley's 1974 novel *Loving Her* is so important. It is the first novel by a black woman with a black lesbian protagonist. And like all the other texts I discuss in this book, it features an inter-racial relationship. Yet *Loving Her,* on one level, does not appear to be invested in the politics of blackness espoused by Riggs in *Black Is/ Black Ain't* or by the editors of *Afrekete.*

*Loving Her* opens with its protagonist, Renay, leaving her abusive husband, Jerome Lee, and taking her daughter with her. We follow Renay to the home of her lover, Terry. Through a series of flashbacks, we learn that Renay and Terry met at the supper club where Renay is a pianist and their friendship quickly evolved into a romantic relation-ship. We also learn that Renay married Jerome Lee because she got pregnant after he raped her on a date while they were both in college. Eventually, Jerome Lee becomes an alcoholic and physically and psy-chologically abuses Renay. When Renay finally leaves him, she does so for the wealthy Terry, who is a writer. Renay is inaugurated into Terry's upper-class, white lesbian existence, and she flourishes free of abuse and financial worry. Terry buys Renay a new piano and finances the completion of her college education. Jerome Lee, ultimately realizing his wife has left him for a lesbian, aggressively beats Renay (almost to death) and ultimately kills their daughter, Denise, in a drunken driv-ing accident. Devastated by her daughter's death, Renay leaves Terry to heal but ultimately returns to her, and they live happily together.

As Alycee Lane points out in her foreword to the 1997 edition of *Loving Her,* the novel is in many ways a rejection of the sexist logic of the black nationalist movement of the 1960s. Jerome Lee's verbal abuse of Renay often takes the misogynistic tone of a black nationalist invec-tive that saw the black woman's role in the movement as subordinate to men. In a violent confrontation with Jerome Lee, Renay contemplates the way black women are valued only as sex objects for some black men: "Wasn't that what most black men wanted their women for? To take their anger at themselves and the world about them, hold their sperm, spew out their babies?"[9] Women's value, then, in black nationalism as well as in Renay's formulation, lies in their ability to literally reproduce the nation. Yet this desire for the black woman to function as the repro-

ducer of the nation is only a biological one; the black woman is not seen
as a proper voice of the nation, as the appropriate articulator of black
identity. Instead, the black woman is cast as the usurper, cuckolding
black men and contributing to their emasculation, which begins in the
larger, white society. Lane identifies this as the "matriarchy myth,"[10] as
articulated in black nationalist discourse. But the roots of this antipathy
toward the matriarchal in black nationalism has many sources, from
the infamous Moynihan report, to black nationalist discourse, and to
the pervasiveness of the larger, Eurocentric patriarchy which defines
appropriate masculinity in both black and white contexts.[11]

The hyperbolic critique of black nationalism in *Loving Her* is
undoubtedly a tone-for-tone rhetorical response to the powerful black
nationalism at that time, which often forcefully and unequivocally con-
demned feminist notions of womanhood and homosexuality. Published
in 1968 *Soul on Ice,* by Eldridge Cleaver, is notoriously associated with
misogyny and homophobia. In that volume, Cleaver defines "homosexuality" at one juncture as "the product of the fissure of society into
antagonistic classes," and as a product of "a dying culture and civilization alienated from its biology."[12] Here Cleaver is connecting the
black nationalist notion that Western societies are "decadent" to the
existence of homosexuality. Cleaver doesn't have much to say specifically about lesbians, but his tirade against same-sex desire as evidence
of cultural degeneration is inextricably linked to his identification of
same-sex desire as a sign of whiteness. Shockley would have also been
aware of the homophobia of Amiri Baraka and other black nationalists
associated with the Black Arts Movement.[13] Any fair reading of *Loving
Her* must take into consideration the conversation occurring at that
time. What is most clear, perhaps, is that homophobia became one of
the defining characteristics of black nationalism. Henry Louis Gates
notes that "national identity became sexualized in the 1960's, in such
a way as to engender a curious subterraneous connection between
homophobia and nationalism."[14] So *Loving Her* must be read, in large
part, as a reaction to the fact that anti-gay and anti-lesbian sentiment
was "an almost obsessive motif [running] through the major authors
of the Black Aesthetic and the Black Power movements."[15] The novel,
then, is often as vitriolic, reactionary, and simple as was the actual
and rhetorical homophobia of Cleaver, Baraka, and Sonia Sanchez. As
Lane notes, the novel "conducts a 'subtextual dialogue' with black

nationalist discourses on a wide range of issues; indeed, the novel often 'dislocates' them from their 'original context' and reframes them 'in an alien fictional context.' By so doing, *Loving Her* exposes the sexist contradiction in black nationalist utterances."[16] *Loving Her* contests the idea of blackness as male and as heterosexual and is audacious enough to stage the very set of circumstances (the interracial same-sex romance) that black nationalism decries. In this way, the novel refuses the black nation.

## (Not) Loving Her

Despite the important place *Loving Her* occupies in the history of black lesbian representation, it is one of the least written about texts in black queer discourse. This is due, in large part, to the way its interracial love story unfolds and to its lopsided characterization of black men, and the black community as a whole.

For this reason, it is rarely commented on, and has received harsh criticism not only from black nationalists (with sexist and homophobic agendas) but also from black feminist critics, who found themselves drawing away from this landmark work. Writing in 1974, Jeanne Cordova recognizes the author's "nobility of purpose and theme,"[17] but criticizes its failure to deal with the political complexity of same-sex and interracial desire. Beverly Smith also derides the novel for its lack of political analysis of racism and homophobia. More generous critics, like Alice Walker and Jewelle Gomez, hail the novel as valuable because of its landmark status.[18] But Shockley's novel has also been criticized by the same group of sexist writers who lambasted Walker, Toni Morrison, and Ntozake Shange for their "negative" portrayals of black men. Another reason, perhaps, for the dearth of attention to Shockley's novel might be what Alycee Lane calls its "formal weaknesses."[19] Lisa Walker, however, explains that the perception of the novel as rife with stylistic failures results in a misreading on the part of lesbian feminist critics, who should view the novel as lesbian pulp fiction rather than through the literary and political lens of the lesbian feminist aesthetic which became popular in the late 1970s.[20] Walker's reading of *Loving Her* takes what appear to be failures of form and recapitulates them into stylistic conventions which have fallen out of favor.

Lane's reading of the novel also attempts to recuperate Shockley's novel, though not structurally, but rather through a political reading of its themes. Lane's foreword aptly identifies the crucial rejection of black nationalist patriarchal logic at work in *Loving Her* and uses this to recuperate the novel, which often uncritically represents both intra- and interracial love. What stands out for me in *Loving Her*, in the context of this project, is how much it differs from the other texts I discuss here. Unlike any of the other texts, which (with the exception of *Another Country*) all articulate a kind of nationalist politics, Shockley's novel attempts to present the exact liberal, integrationist vision of interracial love rebutted by Riggs, NdegéOcello, and Dunye. Even Audre Lorde's *Zami*, published a few years after *Loving Her*, represents interracial love and then moves away from it. *Loving Her*, on the other hand, makes the daring move of representing interracial love as its protagonist's saving grace. In black queer contexts this is a questioned move—both now and then.

For contemporary black queer critics, Shockley's novel might seem to feed into the homophobic logic that to be gay or lesbian is to be closer to whiteness. The fact that the protagonist, Renay, is not even consciously aware of her lesbianism until her white lover, Terry, "awakens" it within is clearly problematic. It seems to imply that homosexuality is "outside" of blackness and antithetical to "authentic" or "true" blackness. Furthermore *Loving Her* represents the black community as a monolith, where compulsory heterosexuality and sexism exclusively govern black different-sex relationships. Therefore Shockley's uncritical portrayal of Renay and Terry's relationship puts the novel entirely at odds with the queer black nationalist logic present in almost all black gay and lesbian texts that follow it. Consider Marlon Ross's essay "Some Glances at the Black Fag: Race, Same-Sex Desire, and Cultural Belonging." In this essay, Ross asserts repeatedly that

> when an open and autonomous culture of gays and lesbians began to form in America's urban centers during the late 1960's, there already existed largely integrated within the African American community an established and visible tradition of homosexuality.[21]

Given Ross's insights here, *Loving Her* would have to be more invested in a politics of "open and autonomous" mainstream gay identity, which is more post-Stonewall than pulp fiction. There is no reference in *Loving Her* to the way gay and lesbian subjects living within the black community changed the *politics* (if not the practice) of what it meant to be African American.

What makes Shockley's portrayal of the black community problematic is not that she identifies its homophobia and sexism, but rather that she reads *everything* about the black community through this lens. There is no space for Renay within the black community to express her "true" self, which erases the fact that the black community comprises both straight and "queer" subjects. Ross comments on this perception of black homophobia: "The media tends to characterize blacks as being more homophobic than nonblacks—an astonishing conclusion, considering the history of relatively greater tolerance within the African American community."[22] To some extent, *Loving Her* plays to this mainstream exaggeration, presenting the black community as a place that has never contained—and never will—the black gay or lesbian subject. This is expressed overtly in the novel when Renay meets a black gay man who tells her, speaking about his difficulty in finding a black male lover: "I don't believe there can or ever will be gentleness among black men."[23] Yet many black critics write often and explicitly against this notion of the black community. In a published conversation between Jewelle Gomez and Barbara Smith, Gomez comments:

> As far as I can tell, homosexuality has always been an intrinsic part of the black community. When I was growing up everyone always knew who was gay. When the guys came to my father's bar, I knew which ones were gay. It was clear as day . . . It was a community in which people did not talk about who was gay, but I knew who the lesbians were.[24]

This sense of same-sex desire as "intrinsically" embedded in the African American community is missing in *Loving Her*. This acceptance of black queers was portrayed in George C. Wolfe's 2005 film *Lackawanna Blues*. Set in a boardinghouse, it included an openly gay and butch lesbian, Ricky, whose sexuality is known and accepted by the other people in the boardinghouse and in the community. Absent an interracial theme, there is no suggestion in the film that Ricky's lesbianism operates to make her an outsider. Of course it is also true that Ricky's place in the black community is not only her choice, but at the time *Lackawanna Blues* is set, in the 1960s, segregation ensured that all black subjects, regardless of sexual preference, remained within their own communities. But the representation of a black community that is entirely hostile to black queers is a narrative that later films like *Lackawanna Blues* contest in much the same way Gomez and Smith do.

*Loving Her* constructs Renay's relationship to almost all of the black characters (with the exception of her mother and Mrs. Sims, her piano teacher from childhood, who she later suspects is a closeted lesbian) in negative terms. And though Renay is oppressed as a black lesbian, she has no sense of solidarity with other black women in the novel. As much as the novel (rightfully) critiques the sexism and homophobia of the black community, it does little to make a distinction between the black community and black nationalism. Even black women, who have as much interest in combating sexism and abuse as Renay does, are not sympathetically rendered in the novel. In thinking about her best friend, Fran (who encourages her to leave the abusive Jerome Lee), Renay decides she cannot tell her about Terry: "Fran would never be able to understand her loving a woman as Fran loved a man."[25] Then Renay quickly moves to essentialize Fran into "the" black woman:

> Black women were the most vehement about women loving each other. This kind of love was worse to them than the acts of adultery or incest, for it was homophile. It was worse than being inflicted with an incurable disease. Black women could be sympathetic about illegitimacy, raising the children of others, having affairs with married men—but not toward Lesbianism, which many blamed on white women . . . But most black women feared and abhorred Lesbianism more than rape.[26]

This lack of distinction or nuance regarding the black community is problematic because it fails to represent black people in all their complexity; there is certainly no redemption for black men in *Loving Her* and little redemption for the black community at large. And though Shockley critiques the white lesbian community as well, she is far less critical of it as an *impossible space* for the black woman than she is of the black community.

Shockley's portrayal of Jerome Lee is not problematic because it unflinchingly represents the brutality some black women have experienced at the hands of black men, for groundbreaking texts like *The Color Purple* (1982) and *For Colored Girls Who Have Considered Suicide When the Rainbow Is Enuf* (1975) certainly exposed intraracial sexism. What is problematic about the representation of the sexist Jerome Lee in *Loving Her* is that the novel constantly juxtaposes life with Jerome Lee against life with Terry. For every positive change that occurs in Renay's life as a result of her relationship with Terry, the exact opposite negative effect can be seen in her life with Jerome Lee. Writing about sex, Renay notes, "She was like a dead woman with Jerome Lee. Just going through the motions of living, not caring about anything except Denise."[27] Then later, contrasting this with her sexual relationship with Terry, Renay thinks, "She enjoyed sex with Terry. Now she looked forward not only to the nights but to the days. There was life in life now, and love in its moments."[28] For every oppressive action performed or caused by Jerome Lee, Terry functions as the antidote. Jerome Lee sells Renay's piano—a move the novel represents as a violation of who she is, as an artist, a musician, a person—but ultimately Terry buys her another. When Renay disposes of her gold wedding band, given to her by Jerome Lee, Terry replaces it with one of her own. While Jerome Lee cannot sufficiently provide for Renay and Denise, Terry is wealthy and able to give Renay whatever she wants. Renay drops out of school because Jerome Lee impregnated her through rape in college. When Renay partners with Terry, Terry pays for her to complete her college education. Jerome Lee and Terry come into focus in contrast with one other. The novel makes this connection explicit when Renay thinks: "Does anyone really forget the first time, she wondered—the first meeting with someone who becomes very important in one's life? But in remembering Terry, she had to first remember Jerome Lee."[29] This juxtaposition, of Terry as savior and Jerome Lee as oppressor, fails to demonstrate the complex location of the subjects they represent. Terry seems fairly oblivious to the classist and racist dimensions of her relationship with Renay, and Jerome Lee is utterly unaware of his violent misogyny but rather sees himself as Renay's victim. Yet Renay's response to them is uneven: even Renay doesn't seem to be aware of the problematic aspects of her relationship with Terry, though she is quite ready to identify Jerome Lee as the dangerous sexist he is. This is a counterintuitive move, since rarely has a "white space" functioned as the site of salvation for any black subject.

The novel clearly represents Renay as entering the "white world," and this is made explicit in a conversation between Terry and her friend Vance. When Vance suggests to Terry that her relationship with Renay might be difficult because it is interracial and that Renay might get lonely for "her people," Terry asks Vance, "Aren't we her people? Besides, there are such things as interracial marriages. Or hadn't you heard?" Vance replies to this by saying, "But if you've noticed, either for comfort or necessity, the whites usually enter the black world." And Terry promptly responds with "So—she's entered *my* world. *Her* choice."[30] Renay's location "within whiteness" is fully cemented, perhaps, when after living with Terry for some time she has a violent confrontation with Jerome Lee. At one point, Renay describes him as looking like "a wild black savage,"[31] and he ultimately beats her so badly in this scene that she almost dies. Yet her description of him references her position outside of blackness as she uses racist language to describe how she sees him. It would be a mistake to think that his violence in that moment explains Renay's perception of him as animalistic; instead, this moment enacts the ways in which Renay's indentification of Jerome Lee as abusive metaphorizes into racist allegory about all black men. Hence her fleeing from Jerome Lee also performs her rejection of black masculinity in general.

Renay's dislocation from the black community is enacted not only literally, but also symbolically through the death of her daughter, Denise. It doesn't take much reading between the lines to figure out that Renay feels encumbered by her child. There is little or no intimacy between Renay and Denise, and in the narration of the text, Denise is constantly referred to as "the child." The first thing we learn about Denise is that she looks like her father (which, given how Renay sees him, is not a good thing). On the morning Renay decides to flee her marriage, she wakes Denise, and the text tells us that the child had "dark eyes, so like his."[32] The parallels between Denise and Jerome Lee do not end there. When Denise meets Terry for the first time, Terry tells Renay, "She apparently looks like him."[33] And when Renay finds herself at Terry's door, about to change her life forever, she thinks to herself, "If only the child weren't involved, she thought, looking at the tall, slim woman with the shag-cut auburn hair, breasts small and firm under the white blouse open low at the neck, hips slim in the blue slacks."[34] Renay feels weighted down by this child she never wanted and who looks so much like her father. The novel even suggests that it isn't until Renay is secure with Terry that she is fully able to love Denise:

> There were flashing moments of pain when Denise's smile would image his, and when her eyes reflected the dancing eyes of her father's eyes . . . After all she was part of him, and this would always be present. But the reflection of him in Denise did not bother her anymore. Love had taught her not to hate.[35]

It is Terry's love that teaches Renay not to hate her daughter, who is so much like her father. Despite the changed way Renay is able to relate to her child, this product of rape who looks like her rapist, she is still an albatross for Renay. The child is a permanent link to the abusive Jerome Lee, who will never leave her alone. From the beginning, Denise is doomed to die.

The narrative cannot contain Denise because this would contradict one of the novel's primary aims: to demonstrate the decaying black family as the site of oppression for black women. But because Denise dies at the hands of her father, all of the blame for this "death" lies with black men. In this sense, the novel reverses black nationalist rhetoric in which homosexuality is figured as a "death-wish" (à la Eldridge Cleaver) and read as suicide for the nation. Shockley rejects this notion that same-sex love erodes the black family and puts the responsibility for this erosion in the hands of a destructive black patriarchy struggling to assert itself. It is the black child, however, who finds herself in a conundrum. The father desires her (if only for the continuation of the black nation, as it were) but cannot do right by her; the mother will do right by her, but does not want her. Denise becomes Mama's maybe, but Papa's baby—reversing Hortense Spiller's famous formulation[36]—and dramatizing the oppressive link between mother and child when the child symbolizes patriarchy through the father's "ownership" of his offspring.

Shockley is not alone in problematizing the mother-child relationship in order to expose women's oppression within the black community. Both Alice Walker and Toni Morrison have explored the antipathy mothers can have for their children in subtle as well as overt ways.[37] Yet Shockley's portrayal differs in that she presents her critique of the black community and of black motherhood in relation to an emancipatory whiteness. What Shockley's portrayal of the black community suggests, not only by Renay's abusive husband but also by the death of her daughter, is that there is no hope for the black nation at all. And though other black gay and lesbian artists have severely critiqued black nationalism for its sexist and homophobic logic, none of them have been quite so ready to completely abandon blackness. Marlon Ross speaks to this when he writes:

> For the white homosexual, integrating same-sex desire into one's sense of self meant necessarily leaving one's community behind . . . For the black homosexual, nothing could be further from the

case. Integrating same-sex desire within the self meant finding
a way to remain integrated within the home community while
remaining true to one's desire . . . For the black homosexual, same-
sex desire was a matter of finding a way to reaffirm continuity,
rather than a matter of breaking with a dominant culture in order
to gain a new identity through an awakened consciousness shared
with others of a similarly oppressed status. After all, how could
black gays break with dominant culture, since they had never
been apart of it?[38]

This configuration of black gay and lesbian identity necessitates a different model of understanding lesbian identity than we see in *Loving
Her*. As I point out in my discussion of *Tongues Untied* and later in
*The Watermelon Woman*, both Marlon Riggs and Cheryl Dunye embed
devices of continuity with the black community in their works. *Loving
Her* does the opposite and obliterates any continuity between Renay
and the black community. If Shockley were to present the white lesbian
community with as much skepticism as she does the black community,
her book would seem to expose the ways in which almost every community for the black lesbian necessitates some negotiation. Yet her portrayal of Renay's life with Terry is so idyllic that the novel suggests that
in order to be truly happy, the black lesbian must end up with a white
woman of means. It is clear that in *Loving Her* Renay feels that sexism
and homophobia are heavier injunctions than racism is in her life.

It is, of course, seditious to even suggest in this postmodern moment
that one could experience any "ism" more forcibly than another; yet
*Loving Her* does just that. While the racism of Terry's lesbian clique is
annoying and hurtful, it is by no means the kind of life-altering and
dangerous presence that Jerome Lee's sexism is. This would have been,
in the late 1960s and early 1970s, when the book was written and then
published, a highly subversive claim to make given the emphasis in
black culture on, well, *blackness*. As blunt as Shockley's portrayal is,
it could be read as a kind of experiment that sought to cast sexual
oppression as primary rather than casting race as the dominant signifier of subjugation. Seeing it through this speculative lens exposes
the ways in which blackness, even in texts that speak to gender or
sexuality, functions as the de facto centralizing force to which all other
categories of identity become tied. One can speak about gender oppression or homophobia in black contexts, but blackness itself must be

preserved and maintained. This, ultimately, is the great triumph of black nationalism.

*Loving Her* fails to imagine a black lesbian identity in which black women love each other. Even Shockley's later attempts to represent the black lesbian come under fire. Writing about *Say Jesus and Come to Me* (1982), Jewelle Gomez levels this criticism at Shockley: "The main flaw in Shockley's work is not dissimilar from that of her white counterparts: the inability to place a Black lesbian in a believable cultural context in an artful way. Continued failure to do this denies the validity of the Black Lesbian in literature and history."[39] Though I agree with Gomez in some respects regarding her criticism of Shockley's work, I think there is value in *Loving Her* because it exposes the power of a black nationalist ethos for black people of all sexual orientations, which also by extension demonstrates the continuing force of racism in the lives of black people, as I show in the first chapter of this book. So even as *Loving Her* elides racism and homophobia in ways many critics find objectionable, *Loving Her* metatextually preserves Renay's blackness as an important aspect of her identity. What this means is that *Loving Her* is more invested in a politics of blackness than it at first seems to be.

## Black Is, Even When It Ain't (A Locus of Contradictions)

> One of the myths that [is] put out there about Black lesbians and gay men is that we go into the white gay community and forsake our racial roots. People say that to be lesbian or gay is to be somehow racially de-natured. I have real problems with that because that's never been where I was coming from. And that's not the place that the Black lesbians and gays I love, respect and work with are coming from either. We are as Black as anybody ever thought about being.
>
> —Barbara Smith (emphasis mine)

In black vernacular, when you desire *"to get someone told,"* to make clear to them that they could never achieve what you have, you might tell them that they haven't even *thought* about becoming/doing/being what you are: *You haven't even* thought *about being half the woman I*

*am.* It is a claiming of the ultimate position; it is the height of achieve-
ment. Smith, in the above epigraph, deploys this vernacular strategy
to claim a *more* authentic space of blackness for African American
lesbian and gay subjects. Like Deep Dickollective's "blackqueer than
black,"[40] Smith codes the black lesbian as the ultimate black subject.
This claiming of blackness, this relocating of it within the context of
lesbian and gay culture, is a major concern of contemporary black
queer discourse. *Loving Her,* however, does not seem invested in representing the lesbian subject as authentically black. The trajectory of
Shockley's novel instead moves Renay away from blackness in order to
cement her identification as a lesbian. Rather than pull Terry toward
her community, Renay is content to exist in Terry's "white world."
In the previously cited conversation between Terry and Vance, Vance
offers a final explanation of why Renay may have "chosen" Terry's
white world over her black one: "Maybe because there is no black
lesbian world—such as ours."[41]

Asserting that there *is* a black lesbian world is precisely the point
of many contemporary black queer texts.[42] As Barbara Smith goes on
to note later in the previously quoted passage:

> In fact, the cultural and political leadership of the Black com-
> munity has always had a very high percentage of lesbian and gay
> men. If they want to destroy all Black lesbians and gay men then
> they would alter their history of the race. Though closeted in
> many cases, Black lesbians and gays have been central in building
> our freedom.[43]

Despite the narrative trajectory of *Loving Her* that suggests that in
order to come into being as a lesbian she must extricate herself from
the black community, Alycee Lane argues that the novel contests the
nationalist claim that lesbian and gay identity equates whiteness.[44]
Lane argues that Shockley rebuts this nationalist logic by using the
language of "colorblindness" to describe Renay's relationship with
Terry, hence Lane asserts that "Shockley . . . construct[s] desire as
exceeding and transcending race."[45] Though *Loving Her* attempts to
represent love beyond the confines of color, the narrative functions in
a way to never quite let us forget that this is an interracial relationship.
The insistence in the narrative on the racial difference between Terry
and Renay is precisely what continues to ground Renay in blackness.

In other words, the miscegephor has more racinating power than the naïve integrationist fantasy that the novel portrays.

From the beginning of Terry and Renay's relationship, race is an issue. When Terry asks Renay to play Debussy at the supper club, Renay assumes that the white woman is testing her because she thinks a black pianist won't know classical music. Later, when Renay moves into Terry's apartment, Denise asks Terry, "Is Mommy going to be your maid?"[46] And even Terry's actual maid assumes she has been replaced when she bumps into Renay in Terry's home. These overt examples of race tension and racism that surface in the novel function to define the parameters of Terry and Renay's relationship as interracial. At first glance it might seem that these tensions originate from the outside and that Terry and Renay's relationship is unfettered by the constraints of race. But even in their interactions with each other race arises to constantly stage their racial difference.

One of the most obvious ways this occurs is that Renay assumes all the domestic duties in the house as soon as she moves in with Terry. Her first act upon fleeing her relationship with Jerome Lee is to make a meal. In actual practice this differs little from the way she was expected to cook for Jerome Lee. Though the force of Terry's query about dinner differs greatly from Jerome Lee's abusive commands, the fact is that the domestic space she occupied with Jerome Lee is similar to the one she occupies in Terry's house. The difference is that Terry does not abuse her. Renay's role as domestic is underscored when Terry asks, "What's on the menu tonight, chef?"[47] Ostensibly the narrative goal is to move Renay from a vexed domestic space to a libratory one; yet the history of servitude which marks black and white women's relationships resonates with Renay's assumption of domestic duties. As Gerda Lerner notes in her essay "Black Women in White America":

> Black women have had an ambiguous role in relation to white society. Because they were women, white society has considered them more docile, less of a threat than black men. It has reward them by allowing—or forcing—black women into the service of the white family.[48]

It is easy to read Renay's presence in Terry's home as a "reward," given the discourse of "purchase" within the two women's relationship.

The novel suggests on several occasions that Terry is quite literally "buying" Renay's time. When the women first meet, Terry tells Renay,

"I'm wealthy. I'm used to getting what I want, even if it means buying it . . . I'm one of those women who prefers her own sex and I want you."[49] Later, when Terry buys Renay a piano, Terry tells her, "Besides, now you're here, I don't have to spend my nights in the Peacock Supper Club, getting indigestion from that tasteless food, to hear or see you. Why don't you play something?"[50] So the site of Renay's actual labor—her job—moves from her workplace to the domestic space of Terry's house. When Renay settles into a routine while living with Terry, much of her day revolves around doing the domestic work Terry refuses:

> The days had a pattern. After dropping Denise at school, she would return to the apartment and prepare Terry's breakfast of grapefruit juice, eggs, toast and the strong black coffee Terry liked. There were so many little things Terry ignored. She didn't like to make a bed, cook or hang up clothes. These Renay did while Terry read over her night writing with the FM radio station playing in the background.[51]

These "little things" evoke images of black women working as domestics for white women too busy to do such menial tasks themselves. Renay's role in the house "meshes perfectly with the traditional black servant role."[52] In much the same way that gender functioned to create unequal power relations between Renay and Jerome, so race functions in the relationship between Terry and Renay. With Jerome Lee, it is gender that keeps Renay chained to the stove and the home; with Terry, race renders her another black woman cooking in a white woman's kitchen. Either way, her role as domestic marks her subordinate status to both Jerome Lee and Terry. With the latter, it functions to racialize her and to remind the reader of that *other* history of the black woman in white domestic space.

That other history is directly referenced by Renay, who remembers that her mother worked as a domestic in white people's homes in Kentucky. When Terry's maid, Mrs. Wilby, accuses Renay of taking money left for her, Renay is reminded of her mother's frustration:

> She remembered her mother fuming and fussing when she came home from cleaning some of the white folks' houses in Kentucky. She had been upset by the white woman who would sometimes miss things and blame the colored help. It had made her mother madder than hell, and now it was infuriating her.[53]

Through a series of different yet oddly overlapping experiences, Renay finds herself under suspicion in a white domestic space just as her mother was. And like her mother, she too is "working" in a white woman's house. While the narrative encourages us to view Renay's work in the home as the work of a wife—"Their life together resembled that of a married couple"[54]—such spousal relations themselves are not free of the problematic taint of exchange value and commodity.[55]

While the domestic duties that Renay performs reminds the reader of her blackness, so too does Renay intentionally stage and signal her blackness to Terry. Renay decides to introduce Terry to soul food, cooking a meal of chitterlings, turnip greens, potato salad, and cornbread. She even slips into dialect. When Terry remarks that chitterlings have a distinct smell, Renay responds, "They sho' do!"[56] But Terry doesn't like the chitterlings and Renay tells her, "Don't feel bad. Some of *us* don't like them either!"[57] In this scene, Renay consciously stages her blackness for Terry, performing for her through food and language the ways in which she is "black." She even goes so far as to become native informant, letting Terry in on the fact that not all black people like chitterlings. This scene contests the notion that to be lesbian or gay is to become, as Barbara Smith puts it, "racially de-natured."

Despite the fact that Renay has "entered" Terry's white world, the novel forces whiteness to share the burden of racial otherness. Though Renay insists again and again that color-blindness allows her to love Terry despite her white skin, it is whiteness that is erased by color-blindness for Renay, not blackness. This is a subversive reversal of the usual logic of color-blindness. Lisa Walker addresses this idea when she quotes Ruth Frankenburg on the issue of color-blindness: "As Ruth Frankenburg explains, the logic of color-blindness holds that "people of color are 'good' only insofar as their 'coloredness' can be bracketed and ignored, and this bracketing is contingent on the ability or the decision—in fact, the virtue—of a 'noncolored'—or white— self."[58] But it is not Renay's color that disappears in her relationship with Terry. Instead, Terry's whiteness is repeatedly elided by Renay. We are reminded again and again of Renay's blackness, through racism experienced by Renay and by the couple, and through Renay's own naming and marking of her blackness. At one point Terry worries that Renay won't be able to handle "the life" (referring to lesbian life) and that she won't be able to harden herself enough to deal with homophobia. Renay answers by saying: "Terry—you forget—I'm black. We're hardened as soon as we come into this world. It's as if our skin's a hard dark shell to hide and protect all the hurts to come."[59] By answering in this way, Renay reminds Terry of her blackness when Terry seems only to be thinking of her lesbian identity. This statement by Renay is followed by "Funny how she could love Terry so deeply that she did not see Terry's white skin—only knew of Terry's heart and the love in it."[60] Renay foregrounds her blackness for Terry and then erases Terry's whiteness. The rhetoric of color-blindness then, is reversed in *Loving Her,* to render Terry neutral and colorless, while always preserving Renay's blackness.

Through a critique of the rhetoric of color-blindness, Walker argues: "To posit the couples' sameness 'under the skin,' then, is to posit that interior sameness as white, suggesting that Renay is like Terry—and not like Jerome Lee, and most especially not like the heterosexual black women who fall for Jerome Lee."[61] But Renay actually performs and names her blackness repeatedly throughout the narrative, never letting the reader (or Terry) forget that she is black. When Terry tells Renay they must move out of the apartment building, without being told why Renay guesses it is because she is black. "I'm black. Been black all my life, and will be for the rest of it. That's how I know. Good old darky instinct."[62] When Terry tries to define Renay's blackness as an impediment, offering to "exchange skins" with her so she can feel the pain of racism for Renay, Renay rejects the offer and reverses the burden: "No, I like my skin the way it is . . . Besides I wouldn't want to feel as hurt and helpless as you are now inside yours."[63] Renay does not see herself as the same "under the skin" as Terry at all; in fact, their racial difference is never far from Renay's mind. Nor does she believe that Terry's skin is more desirable—instead, she deflects onto Terry's white skin helplessness and pain, expressing desire ("like") for her own skin.

Renay's "skin" functions as the site of knowledge. Without being told why, she knows that it is racism which propels the manager of the apartment building to expel her and Terry. Without having yet experienced homophobia, Renay is aware of the ways that oppression functions to suppress and control people, and she references her experience as a racial minority to suggest that she already has some "tools" for dealing with a new "ism." This might be why critics such as Laura Alexandra Harris argue that "in the US system of black and white *race works queer.*"[64] But in *Loving Her* the converse does not work. *Queer doesn't work race,* which is why Terry's whiteness is elided, skipped over, and erased in the narrative. While, on the other hand, Renay's blackness gives her the will to remain with Terry despite the various obstacles they encounter.

This is a story told from Renay's point of view, and therefore we cannot take lightly all the ways Renay attempts to erase Terry's whiteness. It is clear that Terry sees Renay's skin color. The first time they make love Terry notes that Renay's skin is "so golden brown." On the other hand, Renay's remarks about Terry's skin do not fetishize her whiteness, but rather focus on the ways in which Renay is able to love Terry *despite and not because of* her white skin. Renay thinks, after making love with Terry: "Tracing the whiteness of Terry's skin with her finger, Renay thought, *It is amazing how I can lie here and see and feel this skin and not think of the awful things others of her color have done to us.*"[65] Renay calls her ability to love Terry "unbelievable" because of Terry's whiteness. It is Terry who then introduces the idea of color-blindness: "Darling, love knows no color."[66] But Renay is almost obsessed with color and the history of racial intermixture: "*And yet, my skin is light—tinged with the sun. Someone, somewhere in the past, must have done and thought and felt like this with another— or hated in a different and helpless way.*"[67] This passage demonstrates another erasure of whiteness—Renay describes her light skin as being "tinged with the sun," leaving the miscegenation responsible for her light skin unspoken. In the next line, she cannot avoid it any longer and finds herself wondering about other interracial couplings, forced and consensual, that created her sun-tinged skin. Though Renay has taken a white lover, the text suggests that Renay has an almost adverse reaction to whiteness in general. She loves Terry, but it is not Terry's whiteness that she loves. In fact, she is only able to voice her love for Terry by rendering her whiteness of no consequence.

Renay's aversion to whiteness suggests to me that *Loving Her* seeks to convince a largely black audience that it is possible to love a white person and not be oppressed by her. Shockley directly confronts this audience when she writes of Renay:

> "Blackopaths" would question her capacity to love a white. She recalled the bull sessions in the dormitory when the girls would wonder how Lena Horne and Pearl Bailey could wake up in the

morning to white faces beside them. But now she knew: you can't confine love to color or object. Love is what you see, like and admire in a person, how you feel and respond to that person. Look at her own color and the various colors of the black race. Somewhere, down the line, through rape or consent, body chemistry and mind attraction weren't controlled by society's norms or by the system.[68]

Here Shockley directly hails a black audience, pitching the "capacity to love a white" to a black readership. She also historicizes interracial relationships and points to black phenotypic diversity in an attempt to suggest other possibilities for interracial coupling besides rape. Once again we are invited to imagine blackness ("Look at her own color and the various colors of the black race") while the passage renders whiteness undesirable, as Renay narrates her black roommates' inability to feel comfortable with the idea of "a white face" beside them in bed. Renay's musing also functions to redeem whiteness from this utmost undesirability by suggesting that there is whiteness in blackness, that surely its abhorrence can be contained by the knowledge that most "blackopaths" bear the mark of miscegenation themselves, that they are not as far from "white" as they would like to imagine.

Given Shockley's monolithic portrayal of the black community, as well as the novel's overwrought style, it is easy to miss the ways in which the novel seeks to convince a black readership of its protagonist's abiding "blackness." What is interesting about Loving Her is that it puts the burden of transcending racial difference on the white body, not the black one. We are never permitted to forget that Renay is a black woman; we are invited, on the other hand, to forget that Terry is a white woman. We are asked to see her as extraordinary, as a subject who has overcome her whiteness enough to love a black person. This is a very different state of affairs from the usual narrative of color-blindness that requires the person of color to "transcend" his or her skin and symbolically enter whiteness. Though Loving Her does not preserve blackness in the didactic way we see in Tongues Untied—declaring that black-on-black love is the revolution—it does refuse to compromise Renay's positionality as a black woman. We might read Loving Her, then, as performing a similar function that Hazel Carby ascribes to black feminism: "as a problem, not a solution, as a sign that should interrogated, a locus of contradictions."[69] Understood as a "locus of contradictions" we can see that *Loving Her* works both against and for blackness, deconstructing and reifying it, problematizing and rendering it stereotypically. It is at once a dramatic calling out of black nationalism and a daring taunt to nationalism's anti-interracial stance and also an articulation of black lesbian subjectivity. Ultimately, *Loving Her* critiques the futility of the rhetoric which attempts to silence the black lesbian. Though the novel does not expose the ways in which lesbians have always been within the black community in the materialist fashion we see in other narratives, it does not disavow blackness. *Loving Her* insists upon blackness through the characterization of Renay.

It is not the case at all, however, that among the writers and artists I discuss that Shockley is alone in some tacit desire for the interracial. All of the texts I examine represent and portray interracial love; the difference between Shockley's text and the others is that they seem to be more aware of what a vexed terrain the site of interracial same-sex love is. Unlike Shockley, they do not present interracial love as a site of salvation but rather as the site of an intense struggle around identity. But because Shockley's text goes against the grain of the racial logic governing criticism at the time her novel was published and of the current moment, it can help to expose the ways in which nationalist thought really has become "common sense" in every black community.[70] What a reading of Shockley's novel exposes for the contemporary queer reader is how entrenched nationalist logic is in conceptions of blackness. It exposed a deep need within me to read narratives that offered a vision of the black community as intact; it exposed my desire to see the fracture caused by authenticating discourses healed. Perhaps because it fails to do this in the obvious way it has been largely ignored and passed over; and yet the text's invisibility is not at all due to an aversion to pulp fiction, an aversion to critiquing nationalism, or an aversion to black feminist critiques of black masculinity and black nationalism. We can credit *Loving Her* with turning the miscegephor on its head and using interracial same-sex love to expose the power of nationalist discourse, even in the context of black queer reimaginings of blackness. For what is behind the desire to preserve a "black-on-black love," but a nationalist ethos about race?

The title of Shockley's novel is interesting when we consider that throughout the entire narrative Terry never tells Renay that she loves her. Again and again, Renay says those oh-so-mundane three words, "I love you," to Terry, but Terry never responds with the same. Though the narrative does not consciously question the limitations of this interracial relationship, this small omission seems to. Since the novel is so much about Renay's self-actualization, I can't help but ascribe the "her" in the title to Renay and not to Terry. This book is less about Renay's love for Terry than it is about Renay's coming into love for herself. Perhaps the title of the novel is a call to the straight black community—to love the black lesbian. Perhaps the novel is an attempt to show that Renay is always already within blackness and that loving a white person cannot strip her of it.

# "SHE'S A B*(U)TCH"

## CENTERING BLACKNESS IN
## THE WATERMELON WOMAN

*She's a what? What? What? What? What? What? What? What?*

—Missy Elliott

n 1999, Missy Elliott released her album *Da Real World,* and on it was a single titled "She's a B*tch." While the explicit version of the song spoke the word "bitch," the clean version was released with the second letter of the word replaced with an asterisk on the cover for the single. This was hardly necessary since the word "bitch" is not one of the words deemed profane by the Federal Communications Commission (FCC) and so is not regulated or censored. The effect then, of this asterisk, is a delimiting of the possibilities of how the song is read. Indeed, the word could just as easily be rendered "butch" rather than "bitch," and even a substitution of the word "butch" in Missy's song functions to question the discursive possibilities implied in the open space between the *b* and the *t:* "She's a butch, when you say my name / talk mo' junk but won't look my way / She's a butch / See I got more cheese / So back on up while I roll up my sleeves."[1] It has long been speculated within the hip-hop community that Missy Elliott is a lesbian; blogs like www.rapdirt.com and www.bossip.com openly speculate about her sexuality. And though the exclusionary and nationalist nature of hip-hop might seem to render the articulation of a lesbian identity impossible, Queen Pen collaborated in 1997 with Me'Shell NdegéOcello to record a song, "Girlfriend," a remaking of Me'Shell NdegéOcello's song "Boyfriend," in which the two women rap, "If that's your girlfriend she wasn't last night,"[2] reversing the heterosexual implication of NdegéOcello's original lyrics. Queen Pen is not as well-known as Missy is; being an out hip-hop artist probably does little to help on that front. But if we read the asterisk in Missy's song as a semantic interplay on bitch/butch, then Missy's ambiguous "clean" version of the song marks both what is possible and what is impossible about the articulation of a lesbian identity in the extremely male, heterosexual, and nationalistic space of hip-hop. This play on bitch/butch also requires a particular kind of reader. If we speculate that Missy consciously played upon the possibilities of that asterisk in order to hail her gay and lesbian audience, then she renders a queer reading unintelligible to those not prepared to consider the discursive possibilities embedded within the erasure of that critical vowel. We can read Missy's play on "B*tch" as a queered double invocation, and as a kind of linguistic "almost not quite" play on the speculation about her sexuality. Though the artful use of an asterisk leaves open a queer interpretation of Missy's song, it can also be read as marking the word "butch" as a kind of profane unutterable, leaving an empty space where the lesbian should be.

The problem of erasure regarding the black lesbian is at the heart of Cheryl Dunye's 1995 film *The Watermelon Woman*. What Missy Elliott's ambiguous play on "b*tch" tells us is that the black lesbian can only exist as an allusion in black popular culture. Dunye's response to such silencing of black lesbian history and experience is this "mockumentary"[3] film meant to excavate and explore the experience of being both black and lesbian, then and now. As I pointed in the introduction to this volume, the problem of invisibility is one experienced by all black queers in the fields of queer theory and gay and lesbian studies. Yet even in black queer discourse, it is the black lesbian body that is most absent. Writing in *Black Queer Studies,* Jewelle Gomez notes:

> The invisibility of black lesbians is already an "epidemic" in many academic arenas—black/African studies, women's studies, literature and sociology. The affliction of invisibility is in danger of spreading to queer studies as well.[4]

That the black lesbian is absent from queer studies, even black queer studies, might be most evident by the jacket art on several recently published books that consider black and queer subjectivity, texts, and issues. The very volume in which Gomez's article is published,

*Black Queer Studies,* features the iconic image of a nude, bald, black man, similar to the images that decorate the cover of Kathryn Bond Stockton's recent book *Beautiful Bottom, Beautiful Shame: Where Black Meets "Queer."* Likewise, several other important books that consider black and queer subjectivity privilege beautiful visual images of black men (sometimes in drag), including E. Patrick Johnson's *Appropriating Blackness* and Roderick A. Ferguson's *Aberrations in Black: Towards a Queer of Color Critique.* I am hard-pressed to find a volume or monograph that discusses queer identity in general (suggesting consideration of gay, lesbian, bisexual, and transgender identities) that features on its cover a black woman. Of course I am not suggesting that there should be no images of black men on the cover of books, either. But it is no wonder Gomez characterizes the invisibility of the black lesbian as a "crisis,"[5] as it seems that even in black queer studies, the body of the black lesbian is as absent as the "u" is in Missy Elliott's "B*tch." We might also read Missy's silenced "u" as speaking to the idea of erasure and silence around black women's sexuality—a problem that pervades not only the often exclusionary space of hip-hop, but one that permeates theoretical discourses about same-sex desire in the black community. Gomez goes on to argue, "Only by telling our stories in the most specific, *imagistic,* and imaginative narratives do the lives of black lesbians take on long-term literary and political significance."[6] Coding the black lesbian body in visual regimes is as important as textual ones, Gomez seems to suggest here, and thus, the relative dearth of popular visual images of the black lesbian indicates a continued suppression of that particular subjectivity, even in the very places, such as in the multiple objects of black queer theory, we expect to find her unashamedly represented. Cheryl Dunye's *The Watermelon Woman* works to make visible the history and the body of the black lesbian.

It is almost a cliché to assert the invisibility of the black lesbian. Despite the attention that has been paid to what isn't there, what hasn't been said, and what is too often unseen, as the statement by Gomez suggests above, the black lesbian has yet to achieve the visibility afforded men in black queer discourse let alone in mainstream culture. As one critic puts it, "The conceit of Cheryl Dunye's [film] is that the archive of the lived reality of black lesbian women is so scattered and fractured that it becomes necessary for the artist to weave the historical narrative herself."[7] The problematic that *The Watermelon Woman* addresses persists for contemporary black queer theorists, even some thirteen years after the release of the film. Articulations of a black lesbian identity are relatively few in number in the context of popular culture, but Dunye's *The Watermelon Woman* stands as an important landmark in the representation of black and lesbian subjectivity. Some of the most famous attempts to discuss homosexuality among black women (which I will visit below) in general suppress the humanity of black lesbians through the elevation of race over sex; and some critical responses to Cheryl Dunye's film elevate sex over race.

Because she is one of the most visible black feminist critics, bell hooks's sense of how to understand the way the straight black community responds to its gay and lesbian members is important. Her essay is of special interest to me because the film *The Watermelon Woman* is as invested in black feminism as it is in queer theory.[8] In her essay "Homophobia in Black Communities," hooks attempts to demonstrate that while homophobia is present within the black community, it is incorrect to assume that homophobia accounts for the totality of heterosexual black response to gay and lesbian members of the community. Yet, as Dwight McBride points out in his essay "Can the Queen Speak? Racial Essentialism, Sexuality and the Problem of Authority," hooks's attempt to focus on the spaces of acceptance of gay and lesbian people within the heterosexual black community masks an unspoken discomfort with same-sex desire which is evident throughout her essay. McBride points out:

> We can no more excuse black homophobia than black sexism. One is as politically and, dare I say, morally suspect as the other. This is a particularly surprising move [to excuse black homophobia as McBride argues she does] on the part of hooks when we consider that in so many other contexts her work on gender is so unrelenting and hard-hitting. So much is this the case that it is almost unimaginable that hooks would allow for a space in which tolerance for black sexism would ever be tenable. This makes me all the more suspect of her willingness not just to tolerate but to apologize for black homophobia.[9]

Not only is hooks excusing black homophobia, at moments in her essay her language suggests an inability, or perhaps unwillingness, to recognize and name lesbianism among black women, hence participating in the erasure of black women's sexualities. In the aforementioned essay, hooks writes:

> Recently, especially as black people all over the United States discuss the film version of Alice Walker's novel *The Color Purple* (1982) as well as the book itself (*which includes a positive portrayal of two black women being sexual with each other*) the notion that homosexuality threatens the continuation of black families seems to have gained new momentum.[10]

Interestingly, hooks never acknowledges that Celie and Shug are involved in a long-term relationship. It is not merely semantics to dwell upon the clause emphasized above; while hooks implies that Walker presents a lesbian relationship in her novel, she allows Celie and Shug's relationship to remain an implication rather than asserting it as a fact. This would be hardly noticeable if hooks did not use such awkward language as "two women being sexual with each other." What Shug and Celie's relationship encompasses is far more than simply "being sexual with each other." In another context the writer Toure points out:

> In the straight mind, the gay man is defined primarily by his sexuality, by what he will and won't do with his dick. But, as with any human, the most important and powerful part of the gay body is not below the waist. Politically and romantically, the most critical organ is the heart, which gay men choose over and again, in the face of all sorts of societal rejection and oppression, to open for a deep, intense, self-assuring love with another male.[11]

Though the subject of Toure's comment here is men, the same could be applied to the relationship between Celie and Shug, which is—as Alice Walker and almost all critics writing about *The Color Purple* point out—a lesbian relationship. The vital component of any relationship is not what occurs on the bodily level, Toure suggests here. Hooks's erasure of the relationship between Shug and Celie renders what occurs between them trivial and dangerously vague. To reduce their relationship to "being sexual with each other," represents an erasure of lesbian subjectivity and renders the black lesbian invisible, reducing Celie and Shug to nondescript, sexualized, and objectified female bodies.

In addition to discursively performing an erasure of black lesbians in her essay, hooks links same-sex desire to whiteness:

In one case, when a black family learned of their daughter's lesbianism, they did not question her sexual preference (saying they
weren't stupid, they had known she was gay) but the racial identity
of her lovers. Why white women and not black women? Her gayness, expressed exclusively in relationships with white women,
was deemed threatening because it was perceived as estranging
her from her blackness.

Little is written about this struggle. Often black families who
acknowledge and accept gayness find interracial coupling harder
to accept. Certainly among black lesbians the issue of black
women preferring solely white lovers is discussed, but usually in
private conversations. These relationships, like all cross-racial intimate relationships, are informed by the dynamics of racism and
white supremacy. Black lesbians have spoken about the absence
of acknowledgment of one another at social gatherings where the
majority of black women present are with white women lovers.[12]

In hooks's formulation, the idea of same-race, same-sex love is excluded
as she implies that it is common for black lesbians and gay men to
choose white lovers, erasing the diversity of black gay and lesbian
experience as intraracial as well. Based on one anecdotal piece of evidence, hooks suggests that interracial dating is more endemic among
same-sex couples than it is among straight couples. Hooks's apologist
stance, identified earlier by McBride, not only elides culpability in
the black community for its homophobia, but also enacts the common
elision of homosexuality and whiteness. This formulation links gay
and lesbian desire, in the black context, to the deviance of racism. As
I demonstrate in chapter 3, the idea that black queers are more likely
to date whites than to date other blacks is wholeheartedly rejected by
the critics I cite there. These issues of interraciality figure prominently
in Cheryl Dunye's film *The Watermelon Woman*.

*The Watermelon Woman* is the first feature-length film about lesbianism by an African American. As a "mockumentary," the film expertly
blends several different narrative modes, invoking the documentary
and feature film. Playing a character named Cheryl, Dunye presents us
with an African American lesbian community, comprising herself and
her best friend Tamara (and, peripherally, Tamara's partner Stacey).
Cheryl is a new filmmaker in search of information for a documentary

about a black actress from the 1930s at first only known as "the water-melon woman." The film unfolds as Cheryl works to recover a history of the watermelon woman, discover her real name, and construct a history about her. She ultimately discovers that the woman named as "watermelon woman" in the credits of the films by white filmmaker Martha Page is named Fae Richards (shortened from Faith Richardson) and that she is a lesbian. This knowledge inspires Cheryl to find out more about Fae, and in so doing, she ostensibly discovers something about herself through her own interracial relationship with a white woman named Diana. In the course of the film, we learn that the entire story of the watermelon woman is fiction, and even the old footage shown in the movie is "a phony,"[13] as is all information about anything related to the watermelon woman.

As I pointed out earlier, in her essay "A Cultural Legacy Denied and Discovered," Jewelle Gomez argues in relation to Ann Allen Shockley's writing about lesbians that "the inadequate representation of Black Lesbians among literary characters . . . is a reflection of their social and cultural invisibility."[14] Though Gomez is writing here about the repre-sentation of black lesbians in literature, her comments are applicable to much of the critical work that attempts to think through representa-tions of black lesbians as well as those discursive incursions into the question of the black gay or lesbian person. Some of the essays that discuss the representation of interraciality in *The Watermelon Woman* suffer from an inability to see the cultural context of the film as both black and lesbian. Andrea Braidt, in her essay "Queering Ethnicity, Queering Sexuality," writes that "portraying cross-racial lesbian rela-tionships can therefore open up an otherwise fixed rhetoric of identity. The illusion of sameness that is played upon in many a filmic depiction of lesbian romance can be deconstructed in the portrayal of a cross-racial couple."[15] Here, Braidt is building upon an argument of critic Ruby Rich's. A significant quote from Rich's essay is worth reproduc-ing here:

> Queers have the potential for a different *relationship* to race, and to racism, because of the very nature of same-sex desire and sexual practices . . . [In cross-racial relationships] race occupies the place vacated by gender. The non-sameness of color, language, or cul-ture is a marker of difference in relationships otherwise defined by the sameness of gender. Race is a constructed presence of same-

gender couples, one which allows a sorting out of identities that
can avoid both the essentialism of prescribed racial expectations
and the artificiality of entirely self-constructed paradigms.[16]

Braidt, using this quote by Rich, fundamentally misreads the representation of interracial desire in Dunye's film. To argue that race can "take the place of" gendered difference in gay and lesbian interracial relationships is to essentially equalize race and gender as the same kinds of difference. Rich's statement is based at once on a presumption of essential difference in both racial and gender terms and ignores the fact that, as Judith Butler points out, "lesbian sexuality is as constructed as any other form of sexuality within contemporary regimes."[17] Rich presupposes that such relationships are inherently flawed because somehow difference does something vital and necessary (and desirable) in any (homo or hetero) relationship, thereby preserving a model of something "hetero" as essential to any relationship, if not heterosexual then heteroracial. It is this problematic construction in Rich's essay that enables Braidt to argue that interracial lesbian relationships can "open up an otherwise fixed rhetoric of identity." Braidt sees the relationship between Cheryl and her white lover, Diana, as productive because she imagines that Dunye's film suggests that "the discourse of race is tightly linked with the discourse of sexuality in the plot of the cross-racial lesbian romance, in fact, there is no telling them apart. And this is exactly the queer moment: we cannot talk about sexuality without talking about ethnicity without talking about social class . . ."[18] Yet what Braidt misses is that though Dunye represents an interracial relationship, she does so not to valorize the interracial relationship, but rather to critique it. This is evidenced in the film through the relationship of Tamara and Stacey, a functional, monoracial couple. In this way, the film internally critiques the character Cheryl's relationship with Diana and, ostensibly, black/white interracial relationships in general. And at stake in Dunye's film, I argue, is a nationalist (albeit revised) need to claim lesbianism as black and not as interracial.

Braidt does not note that *The Watermelon Woman* is more concerned with claiming a black lesbian history than exploring the liberating possibilities of the cross-racial romance. Furthermore, she juxtaposes Cheryl (the character) against the black community when she writes: "Tamara's affirmative identity politics come into conflict with Cheryl's 'queer' standpoint."[19] (And is it just me or do bells go off when you see the phrase "affirmative identity"? Doesn't that seem like a correlation of Tamara with affirmative *action* politics?) In this construction, Tamara is coded as "black" (i.e., identity politics), while Cheryl (because she is dating a white woman) is coded as "queer," though both women are lesbians. In this way Braidt aligns queerness with whiteness and blackness with identity, missing the intersection of interests represented in Tamara, as a black *and* lesbian character. In this way "queer" is equated with whiteness, and Braidt's desire to define *The Watermelon Woman* as a queer film is also about distancing it from its blackness, which ultimately has the effect of casting the lesbian out. Her erasure of Tamara as queer occurs because in Tamara's strong articulation of black identity, her lesbianism is masked due to the theoretical difficulty of imagining the black and lesbian subject. Just as bell hooks performs an erasure of the black lesbian, so too does Braidt seem incapable of recognizing the racial and sexual dimensions of Tamara's character or Dunye's character.

The failure to read Cheryl and Diana's relationship in a "believable cultural context"[20] also burdens the essay "Body and Soul: Identifying with the Black Lesbian Body in Cheryl Dunye's *The Watermelon Woman*," by Mark Winokur. Winokur compellingly reads the narrative and filmic technique of Dunye's film, aptly identifying the play in the film between narrative and mock documentary styles as well as cogently contextualizing the film in relation to other texts such as *Zelig* (1983) and *Citizen Kane* (1941). But Winokur's misreading of *The Watermelon Woman* is nowhere more evident than in his analysis of Cheryl and Diana's relationship when he writes:

> In writing a history that does not exist, Cheryl/Dunye must find a way of representing desire that valorizes the romance of the color difference incorporated in the film's soft-core photography of Diana's and Cheryl's lovemaking while rejecting the historical orientalization of the racial other's body . . . In including the de-eroticizing "race film" as part of the foreplay between Cheryl and Diana, she is denying the potential eroticization of the lovemaking sequence between black and white bodies.[21]

The use of the term "soft-core photography" is an auditory echo of "soft-core pornography" so that the kind of de-eroticization of the interracial love scene he argues for here is undone by his own linguistic eroticization of it. Winokur's assumption that the race film is "de-eroticized" ignores the sexual dimension implicit in the scenes from the old movies shown in the film; these scenes are always between two women, and at the heart of these scenes is lack (of the male, in one case—when Fae is playing the servant to a white woman—and in the other case, the lack is racial, when two black women have a violent fight about passing). By inserting the shots from these race films, Dunye suggests the under-lying and implicit eroticization that is unspoken between the "white" mistress and the black servant, while at the same time historicizing the relationship between black and white women in terms of racism. And while Winokur argues that the love scene between Cheryl and Diana "rejects the orientalizing of the racial other's body," the film highlights the difference in skin tone between Diana and Cheryl, employing a common trope in the representation of interracial intimacy, from *Guess Who's Coming to Dinner* (1967) to *Mississippi Masala* (1991) to *Jungle Fever* (1991).

But Winokur's reading of the love scene is hard to buy here because Cheryl Dunye has a different relation to the body of the so-called "racial other," since there is no black other in Dunye's film—indeed, the black female body we see is the body of the auteur, the filmmaker and star of the film, which renders the notion of the "racial other" (read: the black female body) void. In other words, Cheryl the character and Dunye the director can only be read as "the other" if one actively resists the identificatory gaze the film imposes upon the viewer. And given the slippage between all the categories of identity in the film, it is hard to draw clear lines of demarcation between the extradiegetic and the diegetic registers. Cheryl/Dunye occupies every position both within and outside of the film, so refusing to "see" through Cheryl's eyes requires some work on the part of the viewer, an active resistance of the process of suture.[22] The love scene between Cheryl and Diana does not valorize their romance; rather it focuses our attention on whiteness and blackness, setting it against the historical filmic backdrop of slav-ery and color consciousness. The implicit suggestion of their love scene is that most of the time when we have historically seen black and white women's bodies together on the screen, these images have reinforced the black woman's status as subordinate and black skin as insufficient and undesirable. By interspersing these "old" images in the love scene, Dunye suggests that we should perhaps read the current unfolding of sex and desire in the context of racism and oppression rather than ahistorically. This is by no means a valorization of interracial romance, as Braidt and Winokur seem to think it is. Indeed, it is a critique.

Elaborating on his attempt to recuperate the interracial romance in *The Watermelon Woman,* Winokur writes that "it is as if she [Dunye] is looking for a model of interracial desire detached from the (tourist's) baggage of history, a model in which color can be sexually other—erotic—without being orientalized, in which the black woman is equal in and out of bed rather than the abject other of the white woman."[23] Here, Winokur posits one of the goals of *The Watermelon Woman* as the reclamation of the interracial divorced from its problematic historical specificity. This seems to me to be an ultimate misreading of the role and function of the interracial romance in *The Watermelon Woman.* Winokur's continual positing of Cheryl as a "racial other" represents a forgetting on his part that in this film, *there is no other* except a fictional one, embodied by the character of the watermelon woman, whose status as other the film intentionally seeks to undo. Dunye's film destabilizes the power of a master, otherizing discourse by revealing the "real" Fae Richards, by exposing the racist women who attempt to keep her hidden, and by giving Fae a name, a lover, and a biography. The parallel character of Cheryl never occupies the space of other, since she is literally in control of what we see. Much of this film unfolds in direct address, with Cheryl (the character) talking into the camera. In this way, the character Cheryl's filmmaking mimics the extradiegetic parallel occupied by Dunye. The film disallows a reading of Cheryl as the other, by placing her both inside and outside the narrative—as the film's "real" filmmaker, Cheryl Dunye; and as the subject of the diegetic narrative, Cheryl, the video store clerk and emerging filmmaker, and as the maker of the internal diegetic film, which is the documentary about the watermelon woman. By occupying every temporal register possible within the film(s), Dunye creates a circle whereby she, as the director, constructs and functions as our "eye," as we view the character Cheryl, who, often in direct address, gazes back into the camera, speaking back to us. Our gaze is controlled from the outside by Cheryl Dunye, the director, and our gaze is returned, by Cheryl the character. There is no passive "to-be-looked-at-ness"[24] operating in *The Watermelon Woman.* An exploitative scopophilia is confronted and denounced. In other words, there is no black other to eradicate.

Seeing *The Watermelon Woman* primarily as a rejection of a problematic black lesbian other and a recuperation of interracial romance at once misses the political punch the film lands as well as the ways in which it questions its own motives. As Robert Reid-Pharr notes, Dunye's film foregrounds for viewers "how manufactured" her "real black lesbian history" is, undermining all truth claims about black lesbian identity.[25] We can try to historicize our identities, Dunye's film suggests, and fill in the "blanks," if you will, but to do so is to participate in a process of construction that is no more "real" than Fae Richards is. The role the interracial romance plays in all of this is to demonstrate how we construct narratives about ourselves and to what productive use these stories might be put. Like the conceit of the absent history of the black lesbian, the interracial romance is not a "real" thing. Rather, like all the other "art bits"[26] which congeal to produce a narrative about Fae Richards, the interracial romance is a device that dramatizes Cheryl's blackness. Because of her relationship with Diana, Cheryl is forced to have multiple discussions about her relationship and her blackness with Tamara. She is asked to define herself. In the process of telling us a "lie," about a historical black lesbian figure, we learn a great deal about the characters Cheryl, Tamara, Stacey, and Diana and their relationship to the highly vexed categories of "black," "white," "lesbian," "wealthy," and "working class." *The Watermelon Woman* tricks us into believing that it is going to fill a void but then says, "Psych!" right when we feel we've gotten all the facts. But is the hole at the end the same one as at the beginning? The inveracity of the film does not rob it of its power, but rather provides it. What we don't have at the end of *The Watermelon Woman* is a "true" story about Fae Richards. What we do have is the multiple manifestations of Cheryl/Dunye both inside and outside of the filmic text. Dunye's film contests the notion of a single, cohesive identity and places its subject in several places at the same time. Which version of Cheryl can we disavow as false, which can we claim as real? The moral binary implied in false versus real constructions is undone by Dunye's film, and what we are left with is an asterisk rather than an empty space—the implication of space occupied but a refusal to define it as one thing.

It has also been argued that one of Dunye's goals is to "normalize the black lesbian."[27] A more precise statement would be to say that Dunye's film exposes a set of always already normalized relations about black lesbians; it is not that she transforms abnormal black lesbianism into the normal, rather she illustrates the normality of black lesbian life. She accomplishes this by placing the interracial romance with Diana against the "naturalized" relationship of Tamara and Stacey. Therefore, it is not, as Winokur supposes, that one of the goals of *The Watermelon Woman* is to reclaim interracial love; rather, interracial love is used as a device to expose the norms of the black lesbian community. In this way, Dunye's film claims lesbianism *as black* and critiques the interracial (defined in the film as coming with the "baggage"—to use Winokur's term—of racism) as being as difficult for black lesbians as it is for black heterosexuals.

Viewers of *The Watermelon Woman* often miss that Dunye's film hails and interpolates black women—both lesbian and straight—because ultimately the film centers the black woman's experience in order to demonstrate that black lesbian experience *is* black experience. In order to understand *The Watermelon Woman*, it is essential that one read it in the context of black gay and lesbian discourse, where questions of racial authenticity are central to the articulation of both racial and sexual aspects of identity. From a dominant perspective, it is difficult to argue with the productive possibilities of interracial love without appearing to be racist, a subject taken up at great length by Christopher Cutrone.[28] But from the position of the socially marginalized viewer, interracial romance signifies much more problematically and rarely functions as a device of liberation, though an exception to this is Ann Allen Shockley's novel *Loving Her,* which I discuss in chapter 3. What *The Watermelon Woman* represents in terms of its representation of interracial romance is a consideration of the history of interracial desire and then the rejection of it as problematic. As critics rush to proclaim the film's merits because of Cheryl's love affair with Diana (which they problematically read as "more queer" than Tamara's relationship with Stacey), the unarticulated critique of the interracial in the film is missed, and vital questions about why black lesbian history should intersect so problematically with whiteness can never be asked.

## Watermelon City: Where Do You Want It?

> *Philadelphia is burning and water-melon is all that can cool it*
> *so there they are, spiked atop a row of metal poles, rolling on*
> *and off pickup trucks the fruit that grows longest, the fruit with*
> *the curly tail, the cool fruit,*
> *larger than a large baby, wide*
> *as the widest green behind, wide*
> *vermilion smile at the sizzling metropole.*
> *Did I see this yesterday? Did I dream*
> *this last night? The city is burning,*
> *is burning for real.*
>
> —Elizabeth Alexander, "Overture: Watermelon City"

The watermelon woman is from watermelon city. The importance of the city and what it means to contemporary black identity frames *The Watermelon Woman*. In her poem "Overture: Watermelon City," Elizabeth Alexander talks about the "sizzling city," about a city on fire. Her poem is about the members of the MOVE organization who were brutally murdered by the Philadelphia police in 1985. The sign of the watermelon stands in for a history of oppression, an agrarian symbol transplanted to the conflagrant metropole. Alexander marries the ostensible rural connotation of the watermelon to the city when she writes "wide / vermilion smile at the sizzling metropole." The word "watermelon" references an entire history of racial pain. Philadelphia becomes watermelon city because the space it gives black folks to occupy is "narrow, narrow," where everything boils down to "life lived on the porch," and "Hello, holy rollers / who plug in their amps, / blow out the power in the building, / preach to the street from the stoop. / Hello, crack-head next-door neighbor / who raps on my door after midnight / needing money for baby formula, / she says . . ."[29] The word "watermelon" robs the city and the subjects it names of an identity that is specific and self-affirming. To "watermelon" an identity, so to speak, is to plaster over the subject's humanity with the bloody flesh of that strange fruit. The term "watermelon" as a nickname for the woman who is Fae Richards in Dunye's film iterates the experience of an effacing racism.

By giving Fae the pseudonym "watermelon woman," the film grounds the character in a history of black oppression. It is one of the many ways the film seeks to make present the black lesbian's racialized suffering. Compare Fae's "nickname" to the acronym for the lesbian archive operated by white women, C.L.I.T. (the Center for Lesbian Information and Technology). The archive has pictures and information about Fae Richards, but Cheryl's access is limited by the white woman who oversees the archive; hence C.L.I.T. foils relations between black lesbians rather than facilitates them. White lesbian identity, then, thwarts Cheryl's quest to discover as many details as possible about Fae's life. Tellingly, the acronym for the archive inscribes its identity in the female body, referencing a different, but related, history of oppression. But it is not through the white C.L.I.T. that Cheryl can unlock the secrets of Fae's life (yes, I did intend this pun, and the point will be more forcefully made below); it is only through Fae's black life partner that Cheryl finally is able to complete her narrative about "the watermelon woman." Like the city of Philadelphia in Alexander's poem, Cheryl is "burning." She is consumed by a desire to historicize her existence as a black lesbian, and just as in Alexander's poem, watermelon—i.e., the watermelon woman—is the only thing that can "soothe" her passion to know what it means for her to be a black lesbian living in Philadelphia.

The importance of location—urban versus suburban—is evident from the first sequence of the film. Though Braidt says that the opening scene of *The Watermelon Woman* takes place at a bar mitzvah, it is clear that what Cheryl and Tamara are actually filming is an interracial black-Jewish wedding. The first words spoken in the film are by Tamara who, carrying a large reflective lighting device, looks into the camera and asks, "Where do you want it? Where do you want it?" in clear exasperation. These shots build to a semiclimactic moment, as Cheryl and Tamara work to videotape the wedding party. It is significant that the first scene of this film is an interracial wedding. It is a space that Cheryl and Tamara are outside of as "workers" at this clearly upper-class wedding, with class being marked by the classical music that plays throughout the scene and by the servers in formal attire. Cheryl and Tamara, in their shorts and sleeveless shirts, stand out even from the people employed to serve food. Tamara's diegetic question raises extradiegetic concerns about where the film is placed and where it is located. Her question also immediately centers Cheryl as the authority, the eye surveying the scene and in control of Tamara as well as everyone else.

This opening interracial scene is important because it suggests that embedded within the site of the interracial is the lesbian eye. Due to the multiple shots of the people at the wedding, a kind of panoptical enclosure is created as we, the viewers, literally feel that we are surrounded by the interracial scene. By having Tamara ask Cheryl "where she wants it," the film foregrounds Cheryl's position as creator and also makes evident the constructedness of the filmic moment. We enter the black lesbian world of *The Watermelon Woman* at the site of interracial heterosexuality.

Interraciality in *The Watermelon Woman* is an extremely vexed space. Even when Tamara, the first major character of the film we meet and hear, is walking around the interracial wedding, she does so under stress rather than at ease; thus, the site of the interracial is upsetting to her, and this will remain true throughout the film. But ultimately the interracial functions as a means to an end: it is a means by which Cheryl can access the black lesbian history she is in search of. With the money made from making the wedding video, Cheryl will fund her research project, which is to make a documentary about "the watermelon woman." In this way, the interracial functions as a vehicle through which Cheryl passes on her journey toward the watermelon woman, who is also herself. Whiteness, or interraciality, enables Cheryl to confront significant aspects of black lesbian history, namely one aspect of race oppression experienced by black lesbians.

By ultimately rejecting her white lover, Diana, Cheryl writes herself into a more "authentic" blackness. Experiences with racism, both intimately (with Diana) and publicly (with the police), reinscribe Cheryl's blackness. In the scene where Cheryl is harassed by the police, a complex set of signifiers converge to enable the police officers' hostile scrutiny. Initially mistaking Cheryl for a man, the police begin to harass her because she is walking around with a lot of expensive video equipment. She tells them that she's not a boy while they roughly push her against a building. Because the pair of cops is interracial, one black and one white, this scene suggests that it is not only her race that marks her for harassment, but it is also her working-class appearance and her apparent (male) gender that invites the importuners' attention. The incident with the police officers illustrates the "narrow, narrow" space Cheryl, Tamara, Stacey, and all the other black women in the film occupy in the urban Philadelphia jungle. Not only is it an experience that Cheryl's lover Diana is unlikely to have, but it is also one she might not understand. Being wealthy and white, Diana escapes the pressures of marginalization that are an everyday reality for Cheryl and those like her, black women and, by extension and implication, black men. Without rehearsing the narrative of police brutality against black men by recreating it on the bodies of black men, Dunye signifies on the themes of bodily policing which characterize the experience of the underclass. Dunye takes commonsense notions about black urban experience and weaves them through her historiography of black lesbian identity. In so doing, she mirrors a narrative about black urban experience in order to solidify identification with other black subjects.

As I have argued throughout this book, one of the greatest anxieties attending black gay and lesbian artistic production and representation is that of racial authenticity. *The Watermelon Woman* is not immune to this anxiety, and in order to understand all of the complexities of the film, one must read it not only as a "queer" narrative, but also as a narrative that is explicitly about blackness. *The Watermelon Woman* is so much a film about race oppression experienced by black women that it is remarkable the film has not been read more frequently in this regard.[30] One way Dunye hails her audience of black women and filmically breaks down the boundaries between the categories "black" and "lesbian" is by signifying through black women's hair. Most of the women presented in *The Watermelon Woman*, except for Tamara's partner, Stacey, have what black women call "short naturals." This is a low, shaved haircut, the style worn by Tamara and Cheryl in the film. At another filming event, the poetry reading by Sistah Sound, many of the women featured there also have short naturals. Viewers reading the black women's bodies in the film only through the lens of queerness might assume that the short, cropped hairdos indicate lesbian identity, when in fact, in the context of the black community, the short natural references another set of ideological signs.

The political implication of the short natural in the context of the black community has more to do with race than with sexuality. As Kobena Mercer famously points out in "Black Hair/Style Politics," wearing natural hair is often read in black communities as "more ideologically right-on"[31] than hairstyles that require chemical intervention because to chemically straighten one's hair is read by some black folks as disdain for one's natural hair texture and as a sign of one's desire to look more like white people. The way black women's bodies look in *The Watermelon Woman,* and the way the characters wear their hair, is important because "such . . . issues of style are . . . highly charged as sensitive questions about our 'identity.'"[32] The short natural worn by a black woman enables multiple readings. On the one hand, the hairdo could be the sign that the wearer has rejected "straightened" hair as a cultural imposition; it is also possible that wearing one's hair short signifies on one aspect of a lesbian aesthetic. When I wore a short natural between 1995 and 1997, I was read in Atlanta as Afrocentric. When I was in California, my short hairdo often was read as the sign of lesbian identity. Before cutting my hair short, I wore dreadlocks. When one of my professors at Spelman saw me after I'd cut my locks off, she said to me, "What you do with your 'do says a lot about you." (She, by the way, wore a short natural too. And still does.)

Like Riggs's ingenious use of dance in *Tongues Untied* as a double signifier of both freedom and oppression, Dunye's framing of black women's aesthetic choices breaks down the discursive barrier between blackness and lesbian identity. While close-cropped hair in a (white) lesbian context often implies "butch" identity, this is not the case in black contexts. The usual oppositions of butch/femme are thrown into confusion in *The Watermelon Woman* because in the context of an Afrocentric aesthetic, neither Cheryl's nor Tamara's hairstyle is particularly "butch." What separates Cheryl from Diana, and Tamara from Stacey, is not so much their clothing, but their hairstyles. In the context of the black community, those hairstyles signify a rejection of Eurocentric standards of beauty. By breaking down the barrier between black and lesbian aesthetics through the use of black women's hairstyles, Dunye further illustrates the way blackness operates to define the practices and parameters of the black women's lives in *The Watermelon Woman.* But it isn't that the short natural *only* signifies an aesthetic informed by black nationalism and Afrocentricity. It is that the hairdo references both cultural and sexual signifiers and makes it impossible for us to decode or define the origin of intention behind the choice to wear the short natural. It is the perfect symbol for the inability to separate aspects of identity into neat, singular signs. The hairdo's meaning shifts and shades differently depending on the light.

The film clearly signifies on certain metaphors of blackness, specifically in the context of urbanity. In one of the more contentious moments between Cheryl and Tamara, the two women share a joint and a forty-ounce[33] bottle of beer. This scene is such a ubiquitous aspect of contemporary black urban cinema that perhaps it is almost invisible to most viewers. Two black characters represented in this way might seem more aptly placed in the movie *Friday* (1995) or *Boyz in the Hood* (1991) than in *The Watermelon Woman*. What such scenes do is connect the black women in *The Watermelon Woman,* and indeed the film itself, to much of the representation of urban black identity in the 1990s. These characters are incredibly complex. Mainstream images depict black figures who drink 40s and smoke weed as lazy and unemployed (not unlike Chris Tucker's character in *Friday*), but *The Watermelon Woman* recuperates certain urban signifiers of black identity while also showing the multidimensional subjectivities of its characters. Cheryl (the character) is an artist who works hard and is employed (in fact, she has several jobs), drinks 40s, occasionally suffers police harassment, and is also a lesbian. Being a lesbian, the film insists its viewers recognize, is not at all at odds with any of the other aspects of identity that shape and define Tamara and Cheryl.

The film further cements Cheryl's relationship to blackness through its urban mise-en-scène. For example, in the scene immediately following the wedding, there is a montage of Philadelphia with specific focus on its urban areas with a hip-hop-style soundtrack and Tamara and Cheryl debating about the kind of film Cheryl should produce. Tamara urges her to produce a film that is "gritty and urban" rather than the kind of intellectual (and, to Tamara, seemingly un-urban) film she imagines Cheryl will produce. Throughout the film, we jump to these non-narrative shots where we see the metropolitan skyline of Philadelphia, with Tamara and Cheryl dancing in front of the buildings of the city. These scenes serve an extremely important function in the film. They link the filmic space of *The Watermelon Woman* to an entire genre of African American film that is set against the city, a major trope and defining element in African American culture and life. Like *Jungle Fever,* which reminds us at its beginning and end that the entire story takes place in New York City (through the framing action of the delivery of the *New York Times*), so too does Dunye's film constantly remind us that we are in an urban, black space through these sequences which break the narrative flow (they do not function in any way to tell the story) and which are filmic moments in time which situate Cheryl and Tamara in the urban landscape of Philadelphia.

The use of the urban as a symbol places the film in the contemporary genre of African American film in several ways. First of all, it establishes that Cheryl and Tamara are not the middle-class lesbians who live, work, and are distanced from their community because of their class status. Urban spaces contain African Americans and are associated with the black power struggle of the 1960s and 1970s, during which time the Watts riots happened and, more importantly for *The Watermelon Woman*, the MOVE organization was brutally exterminated in Philadelphia. The urban functions as an overdetermined signifier in African American culture; it is at once the space of chaos as well as a location of black culture, and it is quite often read as the most "authentic" site of black identity. The black urban gave birth to hip-hop and functions at once as an oppressive containment of African Americans and as a safe refuge from whiteness. More than any other setting in recent cinematic representation, the urban space has become the site of "authentic" African American experience.[34]

Because of this, Dunye's use of the urban in *The Watermelon Woman* situates the characters in black culture. This is even clearer when we consider the film's consistent marking of space. The first thing we see in the film is white text on a black screen: Bryn Mawr, PA. Immediately, we know that we are in the suburbs with Cheryl and Tamara as they film the interracial wedding scene. In this way, the film constantly marks its location, hence demonstrating the importance of the city as a figure in the narrative of the film. While connecting the film to the cinematic practices of Dunye's male and mainstream contemporaries (like Spike Lee, John Singleton, and John Hughes), the use of the urban also encourages us to read the film from the perspective of a member of the black urban landscape. The film works to constantly situate not only Tamara and Cheryl within a "black" space, but also to situate the viewers within this space.

Reading from within this black space the relationship between Diana and Cheryl can more easily be discerned as problematic, and all the black characters (including Cheryl herself) say so. Cheryl indicates that she feels "set up" by Diana when they meet at Diana's apartment for the first time. Furthermore, both Stacey and Tamara tell Cheryl that Diana "loves chocolate," which suggests that she sees Cheryl primarily as a black body, not as an individual. Diana's appetite for blackness clearly motivates her to seduce Cheryl. Yet her unwillingness to confront racism in the white community and her lack of a critical stance toward her own desire for blackness all make her unsuitable. Despite the seemingly negative place the interracial relationship occupies, both between Cheryl and Diana and between Fae and Martha, these relationships are productive in that they inaugurate racial self-discovery for Cheryl and, by implication, for Fae.

Furthermore, the film raises the question of whether or not the interracial relationships in the film are entirely optional for the black women. After Cheryl indicates that she feels "set up" by Diana's seduction, the two women sit next to one another and talk. Diana tells Cheryl she is attracted to her and Cheryl replies, "You're a cutie." Before Cheryl can go on, Diana says, "I know. I heard your friend." Diana has overheard Tamara say, "She's cute for a white girl." Here again, Diana takes control of the situation, and before Cheryl can talk, she says, "Now that we have established that we are attracted to one another, shouldn't we kiss?" And again, Cheryl is silenced by Diana as she leans in and kisses her. I am not suggesting here that Cheryl has no choice; rather, I am demonstrating that initially Cheryl never pursues Diana and that she allows Diana to dominate their relationship. It is later implied that Fae only becomes involved with Martha because she wants to get into Hollywood movies. Dunye's film suggests that the erotic attraction between black and white women is heavily influenced by power dynamics, and in both cases white women function as the aggressors in their relationships with black women.

The idea that black gay and lesbian subjects sometimes seek sexual refuge in white lovers (as is suggested by Marlon Riggs's *Tongues Untied*) is not at all what *The Watermelon Woman* presents. Cheryl's involvement with Diana is not about seeking refuge from the homophobia of the black community; indeed, Cheryl is out to her mother and participates in an active and vibrant black lesbian community. Instead, the relationship between Cheryl and Diana arises largely out of Diana's desire for Cheryl, Diana's machinations, and Cheryl's willingness to passively accept Diana as a lover. In the scene immediately following her hookup with Diana, Cheryl says she is "shocked." This speaks to the character's unease with the relationship and marks it from the very beginning as vexed. She also connects her relationship with Diana to the film project, which demonstrates that it is tied to her investigation of the watermelon woman. In other words, the representation of her relationship with Diana is not about the productive space of interracial love or an attempt to parallel the liberalism of interraciality with lesbianism. It is, instead, just another way that Cheryl must walk in Fae's shoes in order to demonstrate the negative impact white desire for black bodies has on black women.

Like Marlon Riggs's *Tongues Untied,* which ends with the decree "Black men loving Black men is the revolutionary act," *The Watermelon Woman* ends with a circling of the wagons. While not declaring it in such a didactic way, the film implies it through the eventual dissolution of Diana and Cheryl's relationship, which occurs after Cheryl's discovery that she is just one in a long line of Diana's black lovers, and through the fact that Fae Richards, known in the dominant history as "the watermelon woman," lived out the rest of her life with a black partner. Through the devices of the inner-city, working-class life, black women's aesthetic choices, and an ultimate disavowal of the interracial, Dunye inscribes the black lesbian as the "authentic" black subject. As such, the *Watermelon Woman*—like Missy Elliott's "B*tch," artfully exposes the presence of the black lesbian in the context of multiple discourses which attempt to silence her.

# EPILOGUE

## READING ROBERT REID-PHARR

I t was James Baldwin who led me to Robert Reid-Pharr. I took a single-author class in graduate school on Baldwin, and he occupied my mind, my dreams, and my feelings for weeks. Reading *Another Country* was fascinating to me because it got to my belief in the interconnectedness of our various desires and oppressions. It is a lesson that some in the class dismissed as Baldwin's embarrassing humanism, but it is one that many of us have yet to learn.

I live in Cincinnati, Ohio, which until 2004 was the only city in the United States that had a law which enabled gay and lesbian people to be denied employment or housing based on their sexual preference. It was called Article 12. Cincinnati is also a city that is marred by its record of police brutality toward African Americans. The oppression of black citizens by the police was so intense that the African American community organized a boycott of downtown Cincinnati, and for the first several years that I lived here, starting in 2001, many black artists would not perform in Cincinnati because of this boycott. The boycott was led by prominent black religious leaders, and the GLBT movement against Article 12 and other homophobic acts in Cincinnati was led by an organization called Stonewall Cincinnati. Stonewall Cincinnati was, for quite some time, a predominantly white organization and was noted by many black gay and lesbian Cincinnatians as racially problematic. The conflict between the city's black religious leaders, many of whom espoused homophobic views, and the racist tone of Stonewall Cincinnati made cooperation between these two groups—which had so much to gain from working together—difficult. Around 2003, I was invited to help pen a letter to the local newspaper on behalf of a friend of mine, who also happens to be one of the city's most visible lesbian artists and activists. While working with her on the letter, I made the suggestion that we include a sentence which argued that in a city that routinely brutalized innocent black men, it should not surprise us that gay and lesbian citizens were also discriminated against. My friend paused and asked me to further clarify what the two had to do with one another.

A homophobic city, I told her, cannot be a city that values diversity. As long as gay and lesbian citizens and black citizens continue to treat the other as, well, "the other," and to assume that the interests of one community bear no ideological or material relation to the other, racism and homophobia will flourish unchecked. This construction, I pointed out to her, also erased the place of black queers, who belong to both communities. This isn't the point of *Queer in Black and White,* but one thing a book like this dramatizes is that various forms of oppression are connected to, but not the same as, each other. Another friend of mine, of another generation, said to me recently when I was discussing with her the thesis of my book that it is "true" that black gay and lesbian people seem more attracted to whites than to blacks. "This is one of the most pernicious claims my book contests," I told her. Her statement was made all the more ironic by the fact that she has had a white partner for almost a decade. Why is it, I asked her, that when we see interracial heterosexual couples, black folks shake their heads and complain, etc., but when we think about interracial same-sex couples, we see it as evidence of some kind of pathological desire for whiteness? As old as these issues feel to me, especially after working with them since 1997, my conversation with my friend brought home to me that what many of us understand about the nature of homophobia in the black community has yet to become "common sense." Perhaps even more frightening to me is that I don't think I was able to change my friend's mind about what might motivate the argument that black gay and lesbian folks "prefer" whites more than their straight counterparts do.

## Writing and Labor

I do perceive of my work, all of it, as a kind of intellectual activism, designed to procure freedom, to contribute to a conversation to make life better for more folks. But there is something else; there is writing. There is the place of the writer and the act of writing that is here, in these pages, too. It was writing which ultimately produced me as an academic. I have been writing my entire life in one way or another. I had dabbled in every possible genre by the time I was a senior in high school and wanted nothing more than to be a creative writer, an author.

When it came time for me to go to college, I had to put myself through school. I had no loans because, for various complicated reasons, I did not qualify for enough to cover the cost of my fees. I had three jobs instead. I worked myself to the bone and had little or no time for the luxuries college is supposed to afford. Not only was my education a life of the mind, but it was a life of the body. The minimum-wage jobs I had to take to put myself through school convinced me of the difficulties of poverty. A typical day started at 5 AM. I would do whatever lingering schoolwork I had; around 6 AM I'd attempt to cajole my two teenage brothers (I was their guardian) to go to school (they would never go). By 7 AM, I was waiting to get on the bus. As an English major, I'd usually do my reading for the day while I took MARTA, the mass transit system in Atlanta, to the other side of town. To go from where I lived then to Spelman College took an hour and fifteen minutes on various trains and buses. My day would comprise a series of shifts between classes and jobs. African American literature at 9 AM; then tutoring in the writing lab at 11 AM; Latin American women's history at 1 AM, then copyediting at the alumnae journal at 3 AM. History of the English language at 5 AM; then waitressing at a sports bar from 7 AM until midnight. Riding the bus back home around 1 AM, I would be all alone. Walking the short distance to where I lived from the bus stop, there were no streetlights, only bushes and the close southern night. Paper writing, reading, and thinking until two or three in the morning. I had so many jobs in college I earned the nickname "The Jamaican," because of the joke that Caribbean immigrants worked multiple jobs. It wasn't a life I wanted to live after college. Not even for art. Perhaps that makes me a sellout, but I went to graduate school primarily because I got funding to go.

The day I mailed my applications to graduate school, there was a torrential downpour in Atlanta. I was at the bus stop at 6 AM (going to my first job of the day, which was serving warrants to people about to be evicted for nonpayment of rent) with the packets in my book bag. I was coughing and then, later, vomiting. Despite the flu, I had to keep going. By the time I made it to the post office (fever in tow), I barely had energy to complete the task of mailing them. Then I didn't have enough money to mail them all. Two of the applications never got sent as a result. All I wanted was to be able to support myself while writing fiction. I made decisions at this time based on survival; graduate school, with the funding package I received, was a way for me to stop, to breathe, to read, and, I hoped, to write. It feels utterly humiliating to own up to the material realities of my academic history. Why should this be so—when people confess to much more intimate details of their becoming than this?

But I must divulge the difficult story of how I made my way. Because by making a decision about how to survive, literally, I became an academic. Initially, I never thought of the seminar papers I wrote as anything more than a hoop to jump through. I didn't realize then that academics could love language too, that they could nurse a fetish for words and sounds. I loved reading and the debates that ensued in seminars; I even found that I loved working as a teaching assistant, but writing academic essays felt like torture. And if I ever were to get an academic essay published, who would read it? Who would care? What impact would it truly have? Wouldn't it simply be a technically clunky, jargon-laden, overly long, and obtuse treatise about an idea or work that only a handful of Ph.D.s cared about?

In that seminar on James Baldwin, we read an essay by Robert Reid-Pharr called "Dinge." I will never forget the experience of reading this essay. I was writing a paper on *Another Country* and struggling to find a way to talk about something I sensed in that text but had not yet realized. Without a doubt, the argument of "Dinge" is brilliant. But what touched me most was the writing. The sheer beauty and risk of the language strummed something in my (then sleeping) writer's mind. It finally occurred to me that academic writing could be beautiful, germane, and clear. Reading that essay awakened within me a desire to write academic essays, for I figured that if I could find my own voice then I could actually enjoy doing it. Though I have not achieved Reid-Pharr's eloquence of prose, reading his writing opened for me a range of rhetorical possibilities I had assumed were closed to the academic. That essay ultimately became the first chapter of my dissertation (a version of it is in this book) and my first publication.

## I Am a Misfit

From that moment, my love of Robert Reid-Pharr's writing began. How can one not love a writer who can academically deploy the word "fuck"? I am a person who says fuck, cock, pussy, shit, and mutha-fucka with great regularity. I delight in introducing my students to the powerful rhetorical pleasure of actually saying precisely what several adjectives and a discrete noun mean in one simple word: fuck. (My students, I must say, are not always as delighted.) What the use of such frank language suggested to me was that there was a place for me in academe—a place for me in language—that I had previously thought was unavailable. And it wasn't just about the language. My undisciplined voice, my tendency to stray from the paths of decorum, my disrespectful grammar, my resistance to the niceties of editing, are all signs of the many ways I don't fit. I spent many years at Spelman College trying to fit: to be black enough, to be "conscious" enough, to seem as if I belonged to a certain class, to seem as if I valued a certain ideology or aesthetic. This continued in graduate school. Most rookie graduate students spend at least the first year trying to quote Gayatri Spivak and sound as if they are ahead of the theory. I tried to, but it just wasn't me. The truth is I am a bisexual multi-class half-black, half-white girl who never learned how to be polite but who can be funny. I am always inviting perfect strangers with good energy to come on vacation with me. I am always bound to say something outlandish, to get nervous and simplify when I mean to complicate, to use shorthand when I should elaborate, to misspell, or misspeak, to say exactly what I'm thinking when I should proceed with caution. Seeing that "fuck" on the page signaled to me that maybe I didn't need to police myself quite so much. Maybe I could let go and write in my own, sometimes tortured, voice. Perhaps I could embrace myself as the misfit I truly I am.

By the time Robert's second book came out, I was well into my second year at a tenure-track job. I had published an interrogative but personal account about Afrocentricity in *Black Renaissance/Renaissance Noire,* and it had been suggested to me that such writing would not procure my tenure. Robert's essay on the Million Man March, as well as his discussion of the death of Essex Hemphill and "Living as a Lesbian," validated for me the sense that my relationship to myself had some relevant bearing on what we might call "the academic." He articulates what I was feeling then when he writes: "We will clearly fail if we give into the fear that our dreams, our obsessions, our grubby secrets can never be vehicles for the articulation of the universal."[1] So at the end of it all, I am here with myself, made bare for you.

As I read through this manuscript, I am struck at several moments by my own critical investment in blackness—which I tend to think of as problematic. In my reading of *Loving Her,* I am hounded by the persistent self-directed criticism that I am working too hard to "rescue" the text from its problematic self. In both *Loving Her* and *The Watermelon Woman,* I am confronted by how colored my reading of these texts is by race, how much blackness I see asserted in those pages and frames. As a person highly invested in demonstrating the constructed and illusory nature of race, I wonder if my work is at odds with my politics. As Reid-Pharr writes in the introduction to *Black Gay Man,* "I find that, like many of my peers, I continuously use the mechanism of the machine to affect its dysfunction."[2] I would like to say that I have followed the texts and gone to blackness when they have asserted blackness, and gone to "queerness" when they have asserted queerness. But that would be a disavowal of my desire to see the fracture in the black community around sexual identity healed. So like Reid-Pharr, I have attempted to "make peace" with the ways this text attempts to mediate that fracture because it "returns me to the visceral, self-concerned, self-pleasuring bases for much of my activity as a left intellectual."[3]

So at the end of this book what I am left with is words, pages, writing. What Robert Reid-Pharr's work said to me as a student was that academic writing could be used as the practice of freedom—not simply churned out first for the obligation of procuring a degree and later for the procuring of tenure. His work spoke to me because he was willing to take the risk to speak clearly, to speak in a writer's voice, to claim a space for those of us who want to be rhetorically unbounded, for those of us who don't fit. What I see when I read Reid-Pharr's work is a bold fearlessness and nurturing care that exposes an intelligence utterly aware of the possibilities of reaching beyond (and yet within as well) the confines of the categories of identity. I see a willingness there to speak to and engage with the likes of *me*—another writer, struggling to speak (for many, many reasons) into the crowded void.

# NOTES

## Introduction

1. Of course, the idea of dating men of other races, who are neither black nor white, is completely outside the realm of possibility. And of course dating other women is out of the question for this group.

2. Wallace Thurman's *Infants of the Spring* (1932) is the first such novel, and the first representation of black gay desire is thought to be Bruce Nugent's "Smoke, Lilies and Jade" (1926).

3. Black gay and lesbian studies emerged most visibly in the latter part of the twentieth century. Artists and writers such as Audre Lorde, Barbara Smith, Essex Hemphill, and Joseph Beam are the first to have "address[ed] the forces within black culture . . . that have rendered their experiences and sensibilities silent" (Woodard, p. 1278). The use of the term "queer" to describe the work done by black gay, lesbian, and bisexual writers and artists, however, is relatively new. Articulations of gay and lesbian identity and desire extend beyond the last decade—but the sustained and collective study of African American texts through the methodological lens of "queer" studies is fairly recent, as Vincent Woodard argues in his historiography of black queer studies cited below. There are many texts which make up the black queer canon. Among them are the anthologies *Black Queer Studies, Black like Us: A Century of Lesbian, Gay and Bisexual African American Fiction, Brother to Brother, Afrekete,* and *Shade.* Many of the authors and works I cite herein all ably demonstrate that there is, indeed, a black queer canon.

   Vincent Woodward, "Just as Quare as They Want to Be: A Review of the Black Queer Studies in the Millennium Conference," *Callaloo* 23 (2000): 1278–84.

4. Riggs's text differs from the earlier film *Portrait of Jason* in that it was directed by a black gay man. *Portrait of Jason,* which was perhaps the first filmic representation of black gay men available to the American public, was directed and produced by Shirley Clarke.

5. Here I am referencing a term used by Dwight McBride in his essay "It's a White Man's World: Race in the Gay Marketplace of Desire." In *Black Queer Studies,* ed. Mae Henderson and E. Patrick Johnson (Durham, N.C.: Duke University Press, 2007).

6. My use of the term "signifying" refers to Henry Louis Gates's use of it in his book *The Signifying Monkey: A Theory of African-American Literary Criticism* (New York: Oxford University Press, 1988).

7. Up until about 1950, African American literature consistently used the

trope of the tragic mulatto. I will go on to make a more thorough case about the nature of African American literature later in the introduction; the subheading for this section references the title of Shari Frilot's film of the same name.

8. See the work of James Edward Smethurst's *The Black Arts Movement: Literary Nationalism of the 1960's and 1970's* (Chapel Hill: University of North Carolina Press, 2005).

9. E. Patrick Johnson, *Appropriating Blackness: Performance and the Politics of Authenticity* (Durham, N.C.: Duke University Press, 2003), p. 58.

10. Quoted in Dwight McBride, *Why I Hate Abercrombie and Fitch: Essays on Race and Sexuality* (New York: New York University Press, 2005), p. 69.

11. I discuss these discourses of authenticity at great length in chapter 1.

12. Wahneema Lubiano, Rhonda Williams, Dwight McBride, Kendall Thomas, and Phillip Brian Harper are among the authors who have identified the ways in which homosexuality is figured as whiteness. I take up this subject at length in chapter 1. Elucidating this point, Gregory Conerly comments on the idea that blackness is incongruent with gay or lesbian identity in the essay "Are You Black First or Are You Queer?" He writes that the question in his title "embodies a central conflict many African American lesbians, bisexuals, and gays experience in dealing with two identities often at odds with each other." The essay appears in *The Greatest Taboo: Homosexuality in Black Communities,* ed. Delroy Constantine-Simms (Los Angeles: Alyson Books, 2000).

13. I use the term "interracial" most of the time here since "miscegenation" is often understood to mean interracial relationships that can produce offspring. I keep the terms distinct mainly for the sake of the scholarly distinction rather than out of any sense that either is more legitimate in any context than the other. The term "miscegenation" is still deployed as if the ideas (of biological race) that animate it are valid. The word owes its etymology to the Latin root *misce,* which means "to mix," and the suffix, *genus,* which is of Indo-European origin and means "race." Given the biological implication of the terms "mixing" and "race," miscegenation has commonly referred to heterosexual interraciality. Some might argue that given the reproductive implications of "miscegenation," it should not be applied to same-sex interracial relationships. I suggest, however, that we think about miscegenation as a trope and a metaphor, rather than rely on the false logic of biological race. By this I mean that if we accept the argument that race is not "real," then neither is race mixing, and the use of the term "miscegenation" always refers to an *idea* about sex and race. As Eva Saks notes, miscegenation laws themselves helped to "create and enforce the metaphor of race" (Saks, p. 62). In other words, miscegenation created new ideas about race. The term, coined in 1864 by David Croly in a parodic pamphlet about "amalgamation," was created for purely political purposes and therefore already indicates the imaginary and illusory nature of what it attempts to describe. In other words, our contemporary view of race as a construction reveals "miscegenation" to be a messy misnomer, and we shouldn't pretend that it can mark *any* sexual act with linguistic precision. Further support of this is that miscegenation has not *consistently* described the heterosexual. Saks notes in her essay that as late as 1941, miscegenation could mean not only interbreeding and intermarrying of races, but also "cohabitation" (62). If we understand

"miscegenation" as alluding to an ideological construction related to ideas about race and sex, we can use it to describe both hetero- and homosexual interraciality. Furthermore, my argument about the texts I analyze here hinges on the idea that these artists use interraciality as a metaphor to invoke a narrative history of miscegenation in African American artistic production.

Eva Saks, "Representing Miscegenation Law," in *Interracialism: Black-White Intermarriage in American History, Literature, and Law*, ed. Werner Sollors (Oxford: Oxford University Press, 2000), pp. 61–80.

14. I make this argument at length in chapter 2.

15. Michelle Wright, *Becoming Black* (Durham, N.C.: Duke University Press, 2004), p. 3.

16. Michelle Wright's book lays out an argument about the function of counter-discourses as part of the formation of black identity. I am thinking of her argument here as a way to understand the methodological aspect of black queer signifying on the interracial.

17. M. Giulia Fabi, *Passing and the Rise of the African American Novel* (Urbana: University of Illinois Press, 2001), p. 6.

18. Dwight McBride has argued that we could read *Giovanni's Room* as the text which inaugurates black queer studies. See "Straight Black Studies" in *Why I Hate Abercrombie and Fitch*.

19. I do not discuss these works in *Queer in Black and White* because I am primarily concerned with texts that are the "first" of their kind.

20. See Sander Gilman, *Difference and Pathology: Stereotypes of Race, Sexuality and Madness* (Ithaca, N.Y.: Cornell University Press, 1985); Siobhan Somerville, *Queering the Color Line: Race and the Invention of Homosexuality* (Durham, N.C.: Duke University Press, 2001); and José Esteban Muñoz, *Disindentifications: Queers of Color and the Performance of Politics* (Minneapolis: University of Minnesota Press, 1999).

21. See Judith Raiskin, "Inverts and Hybrids: Lesbian Rewritings of Sexual and Racial Identities," in *The Lesbian Postmodern*, ed. Laura Doan (New York: Columbia University Press, 1994).

22. There are innumerable texts which consider the question of interraciality in American literature. Some notable examples are Werner Sollors's *Interracialism: Black-White Intermarriage in American History, Literature, and Law* (Oxford: Oxford University Press, 2000), Naomi Zack's *Race and Mixed Race* (Philadelphia: Temple University Press, 1997), Cassandra Jackson's *Barriers between Us: Interracial Sex and Nineteenth Century American Literature* (Indianapolis: Indiana University Press, 2004), Stephen Talty's *Mulatto America* (New York: Harper Paperbacks, 2004), Joel Williamson's *New People* (Baton Rouge: Louisiana State University Press, 1995), and Karen Weierman's *One Nation, One Blood: Interracial Marriage in American Fiction, Scandal and Law, 1820–1870* (Amherst: University of Massachusetts Press, 2005).

23. This term is taken from José Muñoz's formulation in his book *Disindentification: Queers of Color and the Performance of Politics* (Minneapolis: University of Minnesota Press, 1999). I have taken some liberty and altered the word here for structural reasons.

24. Let us briefly consider the difference between the films *Guess Who's*

*Coming to Dinner* (1967) and *Jungle Fever* (1991). In the first film, the dénouement marks the black man's entrance into the white family; hence the black person's experiences with the interracial exposes an outward trajectory from blackness towards whiteness. In the latter film, the protagonist Flipper finds that he is more "black" after he participates in, then rejects, an interracial relationship. Despite his affair with the Italian Angie, the film ends with Flipper relocated within the black community. We can infer from Spike Lee's narrative that perhaps *Jungle Fever* is as much a commentary on the state of the black community as it is on "the interracial" per se. Flipper's affair with Angie is reduced to a mere "symptom" of the breakdown of the black community, which the film encourages us to equate with rampant drug use. In the black-authored case, the interracial plot functions to relocate the black character more firmly in blackness rather than away from it. In Lee's film, Flipper rediscovers his blackness upon rejecting his white lover; in the earlier film, the black protagonist's acceptance by his white fiancée's family is the happy ending.

25. For racists, miscegenation is seen as a dilution, a pollution of "pure blood," which will result, in their view, in a third, mixed, and inferior type. For the amalgamists, miscegenation is the method by which racial difference (and hence conflict) is suppressed and a "new people" can emerge.

26. I do not mean to suggest that every single interracial relationship functions in this way. I think there are an incredibly complex set of relations governing the multiple manifestations of what we might call "the interracial." I think racial differences between couples sometimes cease to function in ways we might expect in this "liberal vision" I make reference to in the text, but I'm not sure it is possible to feel "less" connected to one's race as a result of the interracial relationship.

27. Frantz Fanon, *Black Skin, White Masks* (New York: Grove Press, 1991), p. 63.

28. Fanon, *Black Skin*, p. 63.

29. McBride, "White Man's World," p. 121.

30. Christopher Cutrone, "The Child with a Lion: The Utopia of Interracial Intimacy," *GLQ: A Journal of Lesbian and Gay Studies* 6, no. 2 (2000): 249–285.

31. Fabi, *Passing*, p. 3.

32. Hazel Carby, *Reconstructing Womanhood: The Emergence of the Afro-American Novelist* (New York: Oxford University Press, 1987), p. 88.

33. See Valerie Smith, "Reading the Intersection of Race and Gender in Narratives of Passing," *Diacritics* 24 (1994): 43–57; and Gayle Walde, *Crossing the Line: Racial Passing in 20th Century US Literature and Culture* (Durham, N.C.: Duke University Press, 2000).

34. The range of black phenotypes is often commented on. See F. James Davis, *Who Is Black? One Nation's Definition* (Philadelphia: Pennsylvania State University Press, 1999).

35. Naomi Zack, *Race and Mixed Race* (Philadelphia: Temple University Press, 1997), p. 97.

36. See Robert Reid-Pharr's essay "Cosmopolitan Afrocentric Mulatto Intellectual," in *Black Gay Man* (New York: New York University Press, 2001), pp. 44–61.

37. I realize this is a controversial statement, especially given the way some black nationalist discourses perceive interraciality as a threat to the race. In chapter 2, I will explore this idea in relation to Eldridge Cleaver's *Soul on Ice*. What I am getting at here is that miscegenation in the context of the black community produces new narratives about blackness itself, whereas in the white community, the evidence of miscegenation can only invalidate whiteness. In the context of blackness, miscegenation can contest or test the boundaries of blackness, but it has not historically functioned to "undo" blackness. In fact, it is quite arguable that American blackness is always already a blackness defined in large part by its interraciality. See Robert Reid-Pharr's previously cited essay for more on the slippage between "mulatto" and "black."

38. I use this date since it is the publication date of W. E. B. Du Bois's *The Souls of Black Folk*. The case has been made elsewhere that Du Bois anticipated postmodern conceptions of race in his groundbreaking work. Michelle Wright makes this case quite forcefully in her book *Becoming Black*.

39. Wright, *Becoming Black*, p. 3.

40. Werner Sollors makes this point in the introduction to *Interracialism*, pp. 3–22.

41. Here I am referencing the assertion that *Clotel* is based on the story of Sally Hemings. Recently, descendants of Sally Hemings and Thomas Jefferson proved their ancestry from the founding father through DNA tests. Until this present moment, then, the rumor of Jefferson's affair with Hemings was a kind of national unmentionable. Now, of course, it has been established as fact, yet it still remains a taboo subject—especially for Jefferson's "white" descendants. Interestingly enough, this now factual history of Jefferson's procreation with Sally Hemings functions to question the racial "purity" of all the Jeffersons, providing an apt lesson about the fallacy of racial purity for all Americans.

42. Reid-Pharr, "Cosmopolitan Afrocentric Mulatto Intellectual," p. 55.

43. Alain Locke, "The New Negro," in *The New Negro* (New York: Touchstone, 1997), p. 3.

44. Locke, "The New Negro," pp. 3, 7.

45. Saks, "Representing Miscegenation Law," p. 62.

46. This quote refers to a phrase of Eve Sedgwick's, but it is quoted in Linda Garber's *Identity Poetics: Race, Class, and the Lesbian-Feminist Roots of Queer Theory* (New York: Columbia University Press, 2003), p. 192.

47. The electric slide is common to many black gatherings—especially those that take place in open spaces. It involves a bending forward with the tap of the toe, then a bending backward with a tap of the heel. A small chasse helps to redirect the body in the next direction and move the body up and back, forward then backward. With a short shuffle-jump step, the direction of the group changes and the same movements are repeated. The dance is performed repeatedly in four directions, like a square dance.

48. Maurice Wallace, *Constructing the Black Masculine* (Durham, N.C.: Duke University Press, 2002), p. 380.

49. Among the best-known literary texts that represent black gay and lesbian characters are Alice Walker's *The Color Purple*, the novels of E. Lynn Harris, the work of Audre Lorde, Jewelle Gomez, Michelle Cliff, Essex

Hemphill, and Joseph Beam, and a case has been made, by Barbara Smith in "Towards a Black Feminist Criticism," to read Toni Morrison's novel *Sula* as a lesbian novel.

50. McBride, "White Man's World," p. 93.

51. Ibid.

52. Reid-Pharr, "Cosmopolitan Afrocentric Mulatto Intellectual," p. 10.

53. Ibid.

54. Ibid., p. 11.

55. Bill T. Jones, *Still/Here with Bill Moyers*, PBS documentary, 1997.

56. Reid-Pharr, "Cosmopolitan Afrocentric Mulatto Intellectual," p. 1.

57. See the quotation earlier in the chapter from Essex Hemphill's essay "Loyalty."

## 1. "Ironic Soil"

The chapter title comes from Sterling Stuckey's statement that the birth of black nationalism is due in large part to the contradiction between the freedom promised in the Declaration of Independence and the reality of inequality in early America: "And it was precisely in such ironic soil that an ideology of black nationalism would eventually take root." I invoke this notion of "ironic soil" here to speak to complicated ways in which nationalism is negotiated in the texts I discuss in this chapter. The first epigraph is from Sterling Stuckey, *The Ideological Origins of Black Nationalism* (Boston: Beacon Press, 1972), p. 28. The second epigraph is from the film *Black Nation/Queer Nation*, directed by Shari Frilot (1995).

1. Rhonda Williams, "Living at the Crossroads: Explorations in Race, Nationality, Sexuality and Gender," in *The House That Race Built: Black Americans, U.S. Terrain*, ed. Wahneema Lubiano (New York: Pantheon Books, 1997), p. 136.

2. See "Can the Queen Speak? Racial Essentialism, Sexuality, and the Problem of Authority," by Dwight McBride, in *The Greatest Taboo: Homosexuality in Black Communities*, ed. Delroy Constantine-Simms (Los Angeles: Alyson Books, 2000); "Eloquence and Epitaph: Black Nationalism and the Homophobic Impulse in Responses to the Death of Max Robinson," by Phillip Brian Harper, in *Fear of a Queer Planet: Queer Politics and Social Theory*, ed. Michael Warner (Minneapolis: University of Minnesota Press, 1993); "Black Nationalism and Black Common Sense," by Wahneema Lubiano, in *The House That Race Built: Black Americans, U.S. Terrain*. ed. Wahneema Lubiano (New York: Pantheon Books, 1997); "'Ain't Nothin' like the Real Thing': Black Masculinity, Gay Sexuality, and the Jargon of Authenticity," by Kendall Thomas, in *Representing Black Men*, ed. Marcellus Blount and George Cunningham (New York: Routledge, 1996); "Living at the Crossroads: Explorations in Race, Nationality, Sexuality and Gender," by Rhonda Williams, in *The House That Race Built: Black Americans, U.S. Terrain*, ed. Wahneema Lubiano (New York: Pantheon Books, 1997); and *Sister Outsider: Speeches and Essays*, by Audre Lorde (Freedom, Calif.: Crossing Press, 1984).

3. Robert Reid-Pharr, "It's Raining Men: Notes on the Million Man March," in *Black Gay Man* (New York: New York University Press, 2001), p. 166.

4. Ibid., p. 167.

5. Ibid., p. 175.

6. Ibid., p. 167.

7. Sterling Stuckey, *The Ideological Origins of Black Nationalism* (Boston: Beacon Press, 1972), p. 6.

8. Lubiano, "Black Nationalism and Black Common Sense," p. 236.

9. From *Black Nation/Queer Nation*.

10. The Black Yellow Pages is a good example of the way in which black nationalism has become "common sense" since the premise of its existence is that black people will want to buy black products in order to support the community.

11. See Fusco's epigraph at the beginning of this chapter.

12. Lubiano, "Black Nationalism and Black Common Sense," p. 233.

13. Reid-Pharr, "It's Raining Men," p. 167.

14. Lubiano, "Black Nationalism and Black Common Sense," p. 232.

15. Ibid.

16. William L. Van Deburg, ed., *Modern Black Nationalism: From Marcus Garvey to Louis Farrakhan* (New York: New York University Press, 1997), p. 275.

17. Van Deburg, *Modern Black Nationalism*, p. 290.

18. See chapter 2 for a discussion of Cleaver.

19. Charles L. Isbell, Jr., "Me'Shell NdegeOcello's Hip Hop," December 1994. Isbell reviews hip-hop regularly on his website, "Homeboy from Hell"; the review can be found at http://www.isbell.org/~isbell/HFh/reviews/059 .nj47.html (accessed August 31, 2008).

20. Mark Anthony Neal, *Songs in the Key of Black Life: A Rhythm and Blues Nation* (New York: Routledge, 2003), p. 15.

21. A good example of this is the album by Sounds of Blackness, *The Drum: Africa to America*. The lyric to the title song says, "Kings and Queens, beat down in the new Babylon called America." In response to such fantasies of a royal past, Essex Hemphill reminds us, in a poem recited at the 1995 Black Nation/Queer Nation conference, that "someone had to clean the bathrooms."

22. By "visible" bisexuality I mean that NdegéOcello is "out" and frequently discusses her sexuality in the press.

23. Diana Collecott, "What Is Not Said: A Study in Textual Inversion," in *Sexual Sameness: Textual Differences in Lesbian and Gay Writing*, ed. Joseph Bristow (New York: Routledge, 1992), p. 92.

24. Black nationalist discourse has frequently been critiqued—both from inside and outside the movement—for its sexist politics. See Elaine Brown's *A Taste of Power: A Black Woman's Story* (New York: Anchor Books, 1994).

25. The use of guns as a metaphor for freedom, for example, is one way that masculinity is/was asserted in black nationalism. This might not necessarily have been the case if women hadn't been relegated to their "prone position" and to doing jobs and tasks like filing and typing. See Van Deburg about women's actual duties in black nationalist organizations like the Black Panthers and SNCC.

26. AnaLouise Keating, "The Intimate Distance of Desire: June Jordan's Bisexual Inflection," *Journal of Lesbian Studies* 4, no. 2 (2000): 84.

27. Neal, *Songs in the Key of Black Life*, p. 13.

28. As Mark Anthony Neal notes, in her subsequent work NdegéOcello rejects Afrocentricity and black nationalism in general. See Neal's *Songs in the Key of Black Life*.

29. Quoted in Neal, *Songs in the Key of Black Life*, p. 15.

30. Collecott, "What Is Not Said," p. 92.

31. Barbara Smith, "Towards a Black Feminist Criticism," in *African American Literary Theory: A Reader*, ed. Winston Napier (New York: New York University Press, 2000), p. 138.

32. See previously cited web page.

33. Mainstream hip-hop is normally understood as being a primarily male genre. See Tricia Rose's *Black Noise: Rap Music and Black Culture in Contemporary America* (Hanover, N.H.: Wesleyan University Press, 1994).

34. See Sander Gilman, *Difference and Pathology: Stereotypes of Sexuality, Race and Madness* (Ithaca, N.Y.: Cornell University Press, 1985).

35. For more information on the butch aesthetic, see Joan Nestle, *The Persistent Desire: A Butch/Femme Reader* (Boston: Alyson Publications, 1992).

36. Lubiano, "Black Nationalism and Black Common Sense," p. 236.

37. This is the title of the group's first album, on Sugartruck Records (2001).

38. Lyrics from this song are from the album *On Some Other* (Sugartruck Records, 2007).

39. From the film *Black Nation/Queer Nation*, directed by Shari Frilot (1995).

## 2. "No Tender Mercy"

1. The remark by Eddie Murphy, which first appeared in *Entertainment Tonight* in 1997, is quoted in Mark Anthony Neal's *Soul Babies: Black Popular Culture and the Post-Soul Aesthetic* (New York: Routledge, 2002), p. 127.

2. Rhonda M. Williams, "Living at the Crossroads: Explorations in Race, Nationality, Sexuality and Gender," in *The House That Race Built: Black Americans, U.S. Terrain*, ed. Wahneema Lubiano (New York: Pantheon Books, 1997), pp. 136–156.

3. E. Patrick Johnson, *Appropriating Blackness: Performance and the Politics of Authenticity* (Durham, N.C.: Duke University Press, 2003), p. 64. I made this argument in a previous version of this chapter in the journal *MELUS* in 2001. Stefanie Dunning, "Parallel Perversions: Interracial and Same-Sexuality in James Baldwin's *Another Country*," *MELUS: The Journal for the Multi-ethnic Literature in the United States* 26, no. 4 (Winter 2001): 95–112.

4. Siobhan Somerville, *Queering the Color Line: Race and the Invention of Homosexuality in American Culture* (Durham, N.C.: Duke University Press, 2000), p. 23.

5. "The Black Panther Platform: What We Want, What We Believe," in *Takin' It to the Streets: A Sixties Reader*, ed. Alexander Bloom and Mini Brieni (New York: Oxford University Press, 1995).

6. By labeling all feminism(s) "white," black nationalist politics instead supports the image of black motherhood as the primary function of women in the "movement." This is another way in which the relationship between Eurocentric and black nationalism is enacted, through a similar sexist politics.

7. Ursula K. Le Guin, *The Left Hand of Darkness* (1969; New York: Ace Books, 2000).

8. It should be noted too that reproduction of slaves can also occur through the importation of more slaves. The vexed relationship, however, between slaves and their own processes of reproduction because of the knowledge that their children would also be slaves is what I am getting at here. Slave owners certainly conceptualized their "investments" in slaves as not only in the slave itself, but importantly in the slave's probable offspring, which was in essence like getting "free" slaves.

9. Warren J. Blumenfield and Diane Raymond, *Looking at Gay and Lesbian Life* (Boston: Beacon Press, 1988), p. 94.

10. Williams, "Living at the Crossroads," p. 136.

11. Audre Lorde, *Sister Outsider* (Freedom, Calif.: Crossing Press, 1984), p. 51.

12. Sharon P. Holland, "Bill T. Jones, Tupac Shakur and the (Queer) Art of Death," *Callaloo* 23, no. 1 (2000): 388. This idea of the masculine as the authentic site of suffering in the black community is one that Sharon P. Holland discusses in relation to discourses of death.

13. For a discussion of the flaws of Eurocentric forms of nationalism, see George Mosse, *Nationalism and Sexuality* (New York: Howard Fertig, 1985).

14. Robert Reid-Pharr, "Tearing the Goat's Flesh: Homosexuality, Abjection and the Production of Late-Twentieth-Century Masculinity," *Studies in the Novel* 28 (Fall 1996): 356.

15. James Baldwin, *Another Country* (New York: Vintage Books, 1960). This is a question that Rufus asks Vivaldo on p. 51.

16. Eldridge Cleaver, *Soul on Ice* (New York: Ramparts/McGraw-Hill, 1968), p. 102.

17. Ibid., p. 105.

18. E. Patrick Johnson, *Appropriating Blackness*, p. 57. For a very good discussion of Cleaver's desire in relation to Baldwin, see Robert Reid-Pharr's "Tearing the Goat's Flesh," cited in note 14 above, pp. 372–394.

19. Cleaver, *Soul on Ice*, p. 103.

20. Ibid., p. 97.

21. Ibid.

22. Ibid.

23. Ibid., p. 99.

24. Ibid., p. 102.

25. Ibid., p. 109.

26. Ibid., p. 110.

27. Ibid., p. 109.

28. Eve Kosofsky Sedgwick, *Between Men: English Literature and Male Homosexual Desire* (New York: Columbia University Press, 1985).

29. Cleaver, *Soul on Ice,* p. 106.

30. Laura Quinn, "'What's Going On Here?' Baldwin's *Another Country,"* *Journal of Homosexuality* 34, no. 3 (1998): 51–65.

31. Kevin Ohi, "Sexuality, Race and Thwarted Revelation in Baldwin's *Another Country,"* *African American Review* 33, no. 2 (1999): 261–281.

32. David Bergman, *Gaiety Transfigured: Gay Self-Representation in American Literature* (Madison: University of Wisconsin Press, 1993), p. 165.

33. Holland, "Bill T. Jones, Tupac Shakur and the (Queer) Art of Death," p. 388.

34. Baldwin, *Another Country,* p. 107.

35. Kathryn Bond Stockton, *Beautiful Bottom, Beautiful Shame: Where Black Meets Queer* (Durham, N.C.: Duke University Press, 2006).

36. Baldwin, *Another Country,* p. 26.

37. Gail Bederman, *Manliness and Civilization* (Chicago: University of Chicago Press, 1995).

38. To some extent, it could be argued, *Another Country* is a staging of race in the bedroom. So while it might be conceptualized as an intimate and therefore vulnerable space, it is refigured in *Another Country* as a primary stage for the enactment of "racial problematics."

39. Baldwin, *Another Country,* p. 132.

40. Ibid., p. 134.

41. Ibid.

42. Ibid.

43. Ibid.

44. Cleaver, *Soul on Ice,* p. 107.

45. Ibid., pp. 13–14.

46. Baldwin, *Another Country,* p. 67.

47. Ibid., p. 68.

48. Ibid.

49. Robyn Wiegman, "The Anatomy of Lynching," in *Journal of the History of Sexuality* 3, no. 3 (January 1993): 446–483.

50. Baldwin, *Another Country,* p. 416.

51. For a discussion of Ida B. Wells, see Jacqueline Goldsby, *A Spectacular Secret: Lynching in American Life and Literature* (Chicago: University of Chicago Press, 2006).

52. Ibid., p. 294.

53. Ibid.

54. Quinn, "'What's Going On Here?,'" p. 52.

55. Baldwin, *Another Country,* p. 435.

56. Ibid., p. 132.

## 3. (Not) Loving Her

1. Catherine E. McKinley and L. Joyce DeLaney, *Afrekete: An Anthology of Black Lesbian Writing* (New York: Doubleday/Anchor Books, 1995), p. xiv.

2. Henry Louis Gates Jr., "The Black Man's Burden," in *Fear of a Queer*

*Planet,* ed. Michael Warner (Minneapolis: University of Minnesota Press, 1993), p. 230.

3. Jennifer DeVere Brody, "The Blackness of Blackness . . . Reading the Typography of *Invisible Man,*" *Theatre Journal* 57 (2005): 681.

4. Frantz Fanon, "The Fact of Blackness," in *Black Skin, White Masks* (New York: Grove Press, 1991).

5. Evelyn Hammonds, "Black (W)holes and the Geometry of Black Female Sexuality," in *Feminism and Race,* ed. Kum-Kum Bhavnani (Oxford: Oxford University Press, 2001), p. 383.

6. Ibid., p. 386.

7. Jewelle Gomez, "A Cultural Legacy Denied and Discovered: Black Lesbians in Fiction by Women," in *Home Girls: A Black Feminist Anthology,* ed. Barbara Smith (1983; New Brunswick, N.J.: Rutgers University Press, 2000), p. 110.

8. Ann Allen Shockley, "The Black Lesbian in American Literature," in *Home Girls: A Black Feminist Anthology,* ed. Barbara Smith (1983; New Brunswick, N.J.: Rutgers University Press, 2000), p. 83.

9. Ann Allen Shockley, *Loving Her,* foreword by Alycee Lane (Boston: Northeastern University Press, 1997), p. 44.

10. Alycee Lane, foreword to *Loving Her,* by Ann Allen Shockley (Boston: Northeastern University Press, 1997), p. ix.

11. See chapter 2 for a discussion of the ways in which black nationalism is influenced by white culture.

12. Eldridge Cleaver, *Soul on Ice* (New York: Ramparts/McGraw-Hill, 1968), p. 177.

13. See E. Patrick Johnson's *Appropriating Blackness: Performance and the Politics of Authenticity* (Durham, N.C.: Duke University Press, 2003).

14. Gates, "Black Man's Burden," p. 234.

15. Ibid.

16. Lane, foreword to *Loving Her,* p. viii.

17. Jeanne Cordova, cited in Lisa Walker, *Looking Like What You Are: Sexual Style, Race, and Lesbian Identity* (New York: New York University Press, 2001), p. 116.

18. Gomez, in the previously cited essay, compares reading *Loving Her* to the first lesbian novel ever published, *The Well of Loneliness.*

19. Lane, foreword to *Loving Her,* p. vii.

20. Walker, *Looking Like What You Are,* p. 117.

21. Marlon B. Ross, "Some Glances at the Black Fag: Race, Same-Sex Desire, and Cultural Belonging," in *African American Literary Theory: A Reader,* ed. Winston Napier (New York: New York University Press, 2000), p. 498.

22. Ibid., p. 500.

23. Shockley, *Loving Her,* p. 75.

24. Jewelle Gomez and Barbara Smith, "Talking about It: Homophobia in the Black Community," *Feminist Review* 34 (Spring 1990): 48.

25. Shockley, *Loving Her,* p. 31.

26. Ibid., pp. 30–31.

27. Ibid., p. 84.

28. Ibid.

29. Ibid., p. 12.

30. Ibid., p. 97.

31. Ibid., p. 131.

32. Ibid., p. 1.

33. Ibid., p. 3.

34. Ibid.

35. Ibid., p. 38.

36. Hortense Spillers, "Mama's Baby, Papa's Maybe: An American Grammar Book," in *African American Literary Theory: A Reader*, ed. Winston Napier (New York: New York University Press, 2000), pp. 257–279.

37. See, for example, Toni Morrison's *Sula* and Alice Walker's *Meridian*.

38. Ross, "Some Glances at the Black Fag," pp. 504–505.

39. Gomez, "A Cultural Legacy Denied and Discovered," p. 114.

40. I discuss this in chapter 1.

41. Shockley, *Loving Her*, p. 97.

42. This is explicitly the case in the text I take up in the next chapter, Cheryl Dunye's *The Watermelon Woman*. It is also the case that Audre Lorde, through *Zami* and other texts, was invested in demonstrating that lesbianism is not foreign to black women.

43. Barbara Smith, in Gomez and Smith, "Talking about It," p. 54. Bayard Rustin comes to mind as Smith is talking here; as a major figure in the black civil rights movement his sexuality was closeted, and ultimately he was "erased" from the official history of black liberation because he was gay. Recently, however, there has been renewed attention to Rustin's life, as evidenced by the recent publication of his writings in the book *Time on Two Crosses: The Collected Writings of Bayard Rustin*, ed. Devon Carbado and Donald Weise (San Francisco: Cleis Press, 2003).

44. Lane, foreword to *Loving Her*, p. xi.

45. Ibid., p. xii.

46. Shockley, *Loving Her*, p. 5.

47. Ibid., p. 35.

48. Gerda Lerner, "Black Women in White America," in *Feminism and Race*, ed. Kum-Kum Bhavnani (Oxford: Oxford University Press, 2001), p. 48.

49. Shockley, *Loving Her*, p. 22.

50. Ibid., p. 12.

51. Ibid., p. 39.

52. Walker, *Looking Like What You Are*, p. 131.

53. Shockley, *Loving Her*, p. 51.

54. Ibid., p. 39.

55. See Jane Gerhard, *Desiring Revolution: Second-Wave Feminism and the Rewriting of Sexual Thought, 1920–1982* (New York: Columbia University Press, 2001).

56. Shockley, *Loving Her*, p. 86.

57. Ibid., p. 87.

58. Walker, *Looking Like What You Are,* p. 135.

59. Shockley, *Loving Her,* p. 37.

60. Ibid.

61. Walker, *Looking Like What You Are,* p. 135.

62. Shockley, *Loving Her,* p. 63.

63. Ibid., p. 64.

64. Laura Alexandra Harris, "Queer Black Feminism: The Pleasure Principle," *Feminist Review* 54 (Autumn 1996): 12.

65. Shockley, *Loving Her,* p. 100.

66. Ibid.

67. Ibid.

68. Ibid., p. 84.

69. Hazel Carby, *Reconstructing Womanhood: The Emergence of the Afro-American Novelist* (New York: Oxford University Press, 1987), p. 6.

70. Wahneema Lubiano, "Black Nationalism and Black Common Sense: Policing Ourselves and Others," in *The House That Race Built: Black Americans, U.S. Terrain,* ed. Wahneema Lubiano (New York: Pantheon Books, 1997), pp. 232–252.

## 4. "She's a B*(u)tch"

1. Missy Elliott, "She's a B*tch," *Da Real World,* East/West Records, June 1999.

2. Queen Pen, "Girlfriend," *My Melody,* Interscope Records, 1997.

3. "Mockumentary" refers to a film which follows the narrative and stylistic conventions of a documentary but is actually a fictional treatment. *The Watermelon Woman* is this kind of film.

4. Jewelle Gomez, "But Some of Us Are Brave Lesbians," in *Black Queer Studies,* ed. Mae Henderson and E. Patrick Johnson (Durham, N.C.: Duke University Press, 2006), p. 290.

5. Ibid.

6. Ibid. Emphasis mine.

7. Robert Reid-Pharr, "Makes Me Feel Mighty Real: *The Watermelon Woman* and the Critique of Black Visibility," in *F Is for Phony: Fake Documentary and Truth's Undoing,* ed. Alexandra Juhasz and Jesse Lerner (Minneapolis: University of Minnesota Press, 2006), p. 130.

8. My construction here contains a flaw, though it is a flaw that follows the logic of hooks's othering of black queers. The flaw is that somehow queer theory is something different from black feminism in such a way that they could be structured as entirely different objects. This is clearly ludicrous, as the widely read and oft-cited essay by Barbara Smith, "Towards a Black Feminist Criticism," manifests a complete undoing of this opposition and arguably lays the theoretical groundwork for what will eventually be called queer theory. Smith's essay is feminist and lesbian, and in fact it breaks down the boundary between these categories. Hooks, on the other hand, in her essay on homophobia and the black community, seems to read gay and lesbian identity as

something always already "outside" of blackness and even the black feminism she supports.

9. Dwight McBride, "Can the Queen Speak? Racial Essentialism, Sexuality and the Problem of Authority," in *The Greatest Taboo: Homosexuality in Black Communities,* ed. Delroy Constantine-Simms (Los Angeles: Alyson Books, 2000), p. 29.

10. Bell hooks, "Homophobia in Black Communities," in *The Greatest Taboo: Homosexuality in Black Communities,* ed. Delroy Constantine-Simms (Los Angeles: Alyson Books, 2000), p. 70 (emphasis mine).

11. Toure, "Hip Hop's Closet: A Fanzine Article Touches a Nerve," in *The Greatest Taboo: Homosexuality in Black Communities,* ed. Delroy Constantine-Simms (Los Angeles: Alyson Books, 2000), p. 320.

12. Hooks, "Homophobia in Black Communities," p. 72.

13. Reid-Pharr, "Makes Me Feel Mighty Real," p. 130.

14. Jewelle Gomez, "A Cultural Legacy Denied and Discovered: Black Lesbians in Fiction by Women," in *Home Girls: A Black Feminist Anthology,* ed. Barbara Smith (1983; New Brunswick, N.J.: Rutgers University Press, 2000), pp. 114–115.

15. Andrea Braidt, "Queering Ethnicity, Queering Sexuality," in *Simulacrum America: The USA and the Popular Media,* ed. Elizabeth Kraus and Carolin Auer (Rochester, N.Y.: Camden House, 2000), p. 185.

16. Quoted in ibid., p. 185.

17. Judith Butler, *Bodies That Matter: On the Discursive Limits of Sex* (New York: Routledge, 1993), p. 85.

18. Braidt, "Queering Ethnicity, Queering Sexuality," p. 187.

19. Ibid., p. 186.

20. Gomez, "A Cultural Legacy Denied and Discovered," p. 114.

21. Mark Winokur, "Body and Soul: Identifying with the Black Lesbian Body in Cheryl Dunye's *The Watermelon Woman,*" in *Recovering the Black Female Body: Self-Representations by African American Women,* ed. Michael Bennett and Vanessa D. Dickerson (New Brunswick, N.J.: Rutgers University Press, 2001), pp. 240–241.

22. See the work of Christian Metz for a full discussion of suture and identification in film. "Suture" is the term used to describe the process by which viewers are lulled into complete identification with the apparatus, or the camera.

23. Winokur, "Body and Soul," p. 247.

24. See Laura Mulvey's essay "Visual Pleasure and Narrative Cinema," in *The Film Studies Reader,* ed. Joanne Hollows, Peter Hutchings, and Mark Jancovich (London: Arnold, 2000), pp. 238–248.

25. Reid-Pharr, "Makes Me Feel Mighty Real," p. 139.

26. Ibid., p. 130.

27. Winokur, "Body and Soul," p. 239.

28. See Christopher Cutrone's essay "The Child with a Lion: The Utopia of Interracial Intimacy," *GLQ: A Journal of Lesbian and Gay Studies* 6, no. 2 (2000): 249–285.

29. Elizabeth Alexander, "Overture: Watermelon City," in *Antebellum Dream Book* (St. Paul, Minn.: Graywolf Press, 2001), pp. 9–10.

30. Laura L. Sullivan is one of the few critics of Dunye's film to actually ground her analysis in a consideration of the representation of black identity. See her "Chasing Fae: *The Watermelon Woman* and Black Lesbian Possibility," *Callaloo* 23, no. 1 (Winter 2000): 448–460.

31. Kobena Mercer, "Black Hair/Style Politics," in *Welcome to the Jungle* (New York: Routledge, 1994), p. 99.

32. Ibid., p. 100.

33. Here I am referring to the common reference to "drinking 40s" in hip-hop, which refers to a 40-ounce bottle of beer.

34. See, for example, the films *New Jack City* (1991), *Boyz in the Hood,* and *Jungle Fever.* For a fabulous discussion of urbanity in the context of the black community, see Mary Pattillo, *Black on the Block: The Politics of Race and Class in the City* (Chicago: University of Chicago Press, 1997).

## Epilogue

1. Robert Reid-Pharr, *Black Gay Man* (New York: New York University Press, 2001), p. 11.

2. Ibid., p. 1.

3. Ibid., p. 9.

# INDEX

*Page numbers in italics refer to figures.*

STEFANIE K. DUNNING is Associate Professor in the Department of English at Miami University of Ohio, where she teaches African American literature, film studies, and literary and cultural criticism.

Ingram Content Group UK Ltd.
Milton Keynes UK
UKHW020641220323
418970UK00013B/767